THE

90

DAY

LIFE

HOW TO LIVE MORE IN 3 MONTHS
THAN YOU HAVE IN 3 YEARS

DR. JEN FABER

The 90 Day Life
How to Live More in 3 Months than You Have in 3 Years

Disclaimer
This is a book of nonfiction. Nonetheless, the names, identifying characteristics and details of events have been changed to protect the privacy of individuals and case studies of the author's clients and students shared throughout this book. Any resulting resemblance to persons living or dead is entirely coincidental and unintentional. This book is designed to provide information, motivation, entertainment and empowerment to readers. It is sold with the understanding that the author is not engaged to render any type of psychological, medical, legal or any other kind of professional advice. The author does not dispense medical advice in this book or prescribe the use of any technique, either directly or indirectly, as a form of treatment for physical, emotional, or medical problems. The author's intent is only to offer information of a general nature to help you in your quest to improve the quality of your life. In the event you use any of the information in this book, the author shall not be liable for any physical, psychological, emotional, financial or commercial damages. The reader is responsible for their own choices, actions and results.

Cover Design: Ryan Prucker
Editor/Interior Design: Douglas Williams
Author Illustrations on page 128 and 129: Dr. Jen Faber

ISBN-13: 978-0-9998461-1-7

For more information and additional resources, visit
http://www.90daylifebook.com/resources.

CONTENTS

ACKNOWLEDGMENTS   v

INTRODUCTION   1

Section 1: REFLECTION   27

    Chapter 1:   Why Impermanence Will Set You Free   29

    Chapter 2:   Mapping Choices   41

    Chapter 3:   Owning Your Consequences   57

    Chapter 4:   Predicting Regrets   73

Section 2: A NEW STATE OF MIND
**   FOR A NEW WAY OF LIFE**   97

    Chapter 5:   Breaking Away from Your
               Comfort Zone   99

    Chapter 6:   Defeating Self-Sabotage   119

    Chapter 7:   Bridging the Present Gap   133

    Chapter 8:   The Art of Getting Selfish   155

Section 3: 90-DAY LIFE PLAN   181

    Introduction: How You Will Transform
                   Your Life in 90 Days   183

    Chapter 9:   Why 90 Days   185

    Chapter 10: Begin with the End in Mind   193

    Chapter 11: The Four Life Areas   199

    Chapter 12: Your 90-Day Life Challenge Plan   227

    Chapter 13: 90-Day Success Principles   261

YOUR TIME IS NOW 272

A SPECIAL INVITATION FOR YOU 273

ADDITIONAL RESOURCES 275

A SMALL ASK 276

WITH GRATITUDE 277

ABOUT THE AUTHOR 279

REFERENCES 281

ACKNOWLEDGMENTS

I'd like to thank you, the reader.

Because you are here, I know you are looking for something different in your life.

Thank you for the opportunity to share my message with you. I hope it inspires you to live more into what you want out of your life and take action on it.

I'd also like to extend my gratitude to every single person who is a part of my life story. I have learned many lessons and grown in so many ways because of all of you. I love you for who you are and what you bring to my life.

INTRODUCTION

"If the path before you is clear, you're probably on someone else's."

— Joseph Campbell

'Who Are You Saying No To?'

My nephew recently asked me to be the subject of a school project requiring him to write a memoir of someone in his parents' generation.

The core of his project was my answer to this one question: "What do you want to be remembered for?"

It came out of left field amidst other questions that were simpler and more instinctual to answer.

But this one stopped me in my tracks, and I sat there stumbling as this 15-year-old sat patiently and curiously, waiting for my answer.

I found myself doing a Rolodex-flip through various moments in my life. My achievements, my failures, my journey, searching for a theme and meaning to it all.

I found myself at a loss, realizing that this one question struck a nerve regarding what I really want to be remembered for:

"To never feel stuck in life and help others feel the same."

In that moment, I realized I had been saying "no" to myself. No to my dreams. No to my deepest desires. No to the person I knew I could become. No to the bigger goals I had been burying in my mind for years. I was more stuck in my life and in my head than I wanted to admit.

A school project for my nephew became a wake-up call for me.

And hence this book, which is about helping people stop putting their lives on hold and start taking action now. It will map out how to reset the course of your life from day-to-day routine to creating your happiness and fulfilling your life goals.

If you find yourself in a place where you:

- feel like there is something more in life for you
- find yourself stuck in a rut
- think you should be happy because you've "made it," but find yourself searching for more ...

Then this book is for you, my friend. I believe the reason why so many people feel stuck and underwhelmed with the direction of their lives is that we take time for granted.

People put off the activities they love until the weekends. They stick their dreams on the back burner because they let excuses get in the way.

They find themselves repeatedly saying things like: "It's not the right time. It's too risky. I'm too young for that. I'm too old for that. I don't have time for that. When I have enough money, I'll do that. When I get done with this one thing, then I'll get to it."

People put off the things that are the most important or exciting to them because they live under the false assumption that there is always "time."

Then they stare at the clock every work week just waiting for Friday to come.

They wait to take the vacations and go to destinations they dream of until they get time off.

They wish weekdays away in a job they hate, so they can enjoy the weekends.

They put adventures, hobbies, and time to do the things that make them happy on hold until retirement.

People do this because it's safer to take time for granted than it is to think there will never be enough of it.

Because of this, we never challenge ourselves to ask the difficult questions.

THE 90 DAY LIFE

What if that time never arrives? What if you fall into the habit of filling your weekends with work rather than play?

What if you never take off time from work because you can never catch up on the work in front of you?

What if when that time to enjoy life does arrive, you won't be able to do the things you've waited so long to do?

What if your life is shorter than you plan it to be?

We avoid these questions because they're easy to avoid and they're difficult to answer.

The reason why more people are putting the things they want to enjoy on hold and feeling less satisfied in life is that they're living for the future, and not for the present. They focus on the day-to-day work, stress, and success — or lack thereof. They look ahead to goals and look back to their past, but forget about the current moment.

Then, the precious moments they have to themselves are typically spent looking at a screen for the latest post, trend, or gossip.

All to rinse and repeat starting every Monday.

People think the formula for doing what they want is to use time to wait for an opportunity in the future, rather than taking advantage of the time right in front of them. So it leaves us distracted. People fill their lives with more busy work and chatter.

4 | DR. JEN FABER

To break this addictive and self-perpetuating cycle, this book is going to reveal how to actually break away from feeling stuck in life to create the life you truly want in 90 days. It will guide you on how to stop letting unhappiness, stress, and life routines become your norm, so you can hit the reset button and get more fulfillment and joy from your life. It will help you reassess what's working for your life right now and what isn't. It will put the focus back on what you want, rather than what you're supposed to do.

Together we'll go from a transformation from living life on autopilot to being in the driver's seat.

Throughout this book, I will address how we overestimate how much time we have, but underestimate how quickly we can create new momentum in our life in an instant. I will help you master how to leverage time in your favor, so it becomes your biggest ally, rather than the very thing that controls your existence.

The deep challenge that this book will address and help you overcome is taking time for granted, because when we do, we take our lives for granted and put off what we truly want. This belief in an infinite future opens the door for the fear, doubt, and procrastination that can take over and stop us in our tracks. It prevents us from action because we cloud our days in routine and stability.

I believe this is the reason why recent studies consistently show that over 50 percent of people[1] are dissatisfied with the current state of their lives, their work, and their relationships. As humans, we actually crave free will. We want to be the masters of our fate, but we don't harness the power we have to actually do just that. More people are stuck in a cycle of unfulfillment, despite having access to more opportunities, information, and ideas than ever before.

Exactly why does this abundance in today's world lead to more overwhelm, stress, and burnout in life?

Because people look at what's outside of themselves. With the opportunities, information, and ideas come distractions, clutter, obligations, and confusion. To break away from this or avoid it completely, you must consider what you're prioritizing in your life. Most importantly, you must evaluate whether the things in your life and how you're spending it are truly making you happy.

During our journey, I will pull together over 15 years' worth of insights and experiences gained from reinventing my life several times over, being on a constant quest to reach a higher level of joy in my life, and helping thousands of others do the same in my work as a coach, mentor, and thought-leader.

This book will show you how to look at life in a completely unconventional way, where you learn to build a mindset of "don't wait" and "why not," rather than "I can't."

By the end of this book, you will have a clear road map to use to break away from how you have hidden from what you really want, to create your life on your terms again. You will be able to stop letting fears and insecurities block your potential, and no longer take time for granted.

If you've ever felt like you've "let yourself go" in your life and have settled because this is just the "way it is," then this book will help you break away from that pattern and start to feel like the architect of your life, rather than just some powerless occupant of it.

With what you will learn in the chapters to come, you will realize how quickly you can achieve the very things you have been putting on hold. Everything that you are, will be, and do can change through the power of choice, and you can create an amazing transformation in just 90 days. If you take the time and make the commitment to apply the tools I've laid out for you, you are about to embark on a life journey that will lead to renewed fulfillment and momentum.

If this is coming across as a wake-up call, it is. Over the past several years, I have witnessed people who have spent weeks, months, even years of their lives stuck in a cycle and feeling trapped in their own lives. It is my beautiful obsession now to stop that cycle, because you are capable of so much more.

There is a conventional way of life that keeps us trapped in day-to-day monotony and mediocrity that isn't what you signed up for. You feel stuck in life because you either don't know what to change, or are daunted by the magnitude of what you do want to change.

So, the day-to-day routines become a habit. Then a comfort. Then just simply who we are. Then life just flashes right past you.

But what if people did the opposite? What if we didn't take time for granted?

What if we remembered that time is impermanent, and life is all too short?

What if you created a feeling of urgency in your life to get things done and start living into your deepest dreams today, a day spent like it was your last?

Think about how different life would feel if we purely chose that level of intent and focus.

Time is not guaranteed, and it is my goal through this book to help you create a new urgency to start living now.

To do the things you've been putting off because there is "time" down the road.

To help you stop putting your life on hold.

To start living into your dreams rather than waiting for the right time to make them happen.

To not wait until retirement to live the life you want.

To stop letting fears and insecurities hold you back from moving toward your potential.

I want to help you break away from how life has boxed you away from the dreams or happiness you've been putting on hold, and start to create your life on your terms again, or maybe for the first time ever.

What Experience Has Taught Us

I've been fortunate to be able to train thousands of people around the world who want to break away from feeling stuck and create a life that they want, and what I've experienced is that more people are feeling stuck in life than ever before.

But people are also hungrier for change. They are seeking new answers, new solutions, and new ways to create more in their lives. They are committed and dedicated to change, and they are eager to reflect on their current lives, so they can understand what has brought them to this point and figure out how to create a new future for themselves. They know that they are a culmination of their life's experiences, and they're looking for ways to channel those experiences into something more meaningful.

Experience is the best teacher, but it is not the first teacher we experience in the beginning of our lives.

We have multiple influences in our life that shape what we think, what we do, and ultimately who we are. Our parents, teachers, friends, siblings, and many others play a pivotal role in shaping our beliefs about ourselves and others — and what's possible.

These early influences teach us about discipline, rules, standards, and how to be a part of society. They teach us what to learn, when to learn it, and how to learn it. We learn to respect others and raise our hands when we want to speak.

We get the first tastes of success and failure in school when we get a good grade or bomb an exam. We learn about core life principles like compassion, understanding, commitment, and acceptance.

Because of this, we also learn the power of listening to and following what others expect of us. It's how we learn.

But within that, I believe we can lose the power of self-discovery, self-reliance, and self-love, because so much of our focus is put on things outside of us —and satisfying others. We aren't inherently taught how to focus on our own potential and power to do great things in the world.

I believe that is the challenge we face as we become adults.

We start to carve our own path in life, but is that path really ours or one built upon these earlier influences in our life?

This is why so many people wake up at some point in their life wondering what they're doing and oftentimes find themselves immersed in a day-to-day way of life that gives no space to reflect on where their life is going, much less even consider change. It's why the mid-life crisis exists and why similar angst is becoming more prevalent throughout our lives. In fact, studies show that mid-life crises are now happening to people as early as their 20s, even though they have their whole lives ahead of them.[2]

Ultimately what we all seek in life is freedom.

That definition is different for all of us, but that is a bond that holds us all together.

In the end, we want to feel free. We want to make our own choices. We want to choose who we want to be with, what we want to do, where we want to spend our lives, and how we want to spend our time.

But we are steered toward a conventional path for our lives that goes something like this: Go to school. Get your degree, then your job. Work and build your career for the next 40-50 years, along the way getting married, having kids, buying a house. Then work hard to pay off bills and loans and plan for 2-4 weeks out of the year when you can take a vacation.

Then continue to work hard. Get lost in day-to-day life, where you never feel like there's enough time and you can't wait for the weekend to come.

But you know deep inside that if you keep this up long enough, the rewards will come, *all in good time of course*. You'll get a bigger paycheck, a nicer house, and a spiffier car. You'll get more vacation once you "put in your time." The dangling carrot that's waiting for you is that blissful stage known as retirement, where you don't have to answer to anyone. Your time and how you spend it is completely up to you.

Quick time out: I'm not here to dissuade you from any of these decisions or anything specific on that path, nor am I saying that any of these decisions are stopping you from living the life you want. In fact, these milestones can provide some of the greatest moments of joy in our lives.

What I am saying is that this path makes people feel like they are at the whim of how their lives are unfolding, rather than creating it. People wait for the right circumstances to arrive, rather than creating the opportunities themselves.

From childhood, most of us are taught to become regimented in our thinking and blindly accept what we're being taught by our "influencers," like our parents or the teachers, bosses, alpha males or females who enter our lives, or the mushrooming media that envelopes us. Over time, this constructs the box that defines what we come to believe life is like. Some parts of this box are good, but others are restricting or ill-fitting.

This is why children can be so unsettling when they constantly ask, "Why." It forces even a momentary reconsideration of our "assumptions" — of elements of the "conventional thinking." But we lose that childlike curiosity as we become adults as the box we have built gets stronger, develops thicker walls, and traps us.

A key part of this journey we're going to embark upon involves reconsidering everything you have known to be "true and absolute," and challenging your assumptions about life, love, job, health, and so forth. I will ask you to look within, so we can reassess and break down the assumptions that hold you back, the ones that have come from a lifetime's worth of external forces, opinions, and beliefs.

Living in the moment also involves living with an awareness that embraces the notion that change is constant, which is why the cornerstone of creating more freedom in your life will be based on impermanence. This is where we will start our journey.

What you know to be true about your life and what you're capable of are about to change. The earth was flat once, and we reconsidered that "truth" as our knowledge grew to discover that it is truly round. Nothing is set in stone, not even stone.

So we're out to discover who you really are, by tearing down the box of what you've been taught and building a new one that you can thrive within.

People end up only focusing on thin slices of time in a given day, week, year, or lifetime where we can just truly be and do what we want. And the worst part is that, typically, we end up spending those thin slices of time on things that really don't bring true fulfillment into our lives.

It's why TV is so popular, so we can get lost in a show and "turn off." It's why social media continues to boom because we seek validation from others, and don't give ourselves the permission to get quiet and actually find the love from within.

We need to turn off the noise in our lives and start to listen within ourselves again.

We need to create a space where we can really ask ourselves: "Am I happy with the way my life is going right now?" Right. Now.

Because what I know to be true is this: If you have a plan where you can make more of your time, where you could take more action on what makes you happy, you will feel freer to live your life in this moment, rather than waiting until the weekend or retirement to do it.

In my years as a coach and mentor, I've seen far too many people put their lives on hold because they listen to the opinions of what others think is best for them, or they're waiting for the right time, the right job, the right amount of money, or retirement to take action. Or they find themselves seeking some magical "system" or some "charismatic leader" to grab them by the hand and march them on a path that's already laid out for them. They look to something outside of themselves to create their life for them.

So they end up following a path that is not truly their own.

If that's you, you're not alone. I, too, have found myself in this position.

We wait for the right circumstances to appear, so we can then take action.

And all waiting does is make you a passive bystander in your life, hoping that something will change to make your life better.

The next 90 days are going to change that for you. You will learn how to step away from your life routines and reassess your assumptions about life, yourself, and what's possible.

My job in this book is not to just give you some rote system to follow. My goal is to give you the framework to discover the life you want and the knowledge to empower yourself to create it.

What Led to Here

Since early in my life, I knew that I never wanted to be put into a "box." I grew up on a dairy farm in rural Wisconsin. My parents encouraged me to move away, telling me: "There's no future in farming." I am grateful for my parents because they taught me to carve my own path.

This lesson has defined me at many pivotal points in my life. It's why I decided to attend the University of Wisconsin, because I knew it would challenge me academically far more than any other state school and provide a culture shock compared to my rural roots. It's why I pursued a doctorate in chiropractic, because that was far more unconventional than a traditional career in medicine. It's why I decided to do my residency in New Zealand, then start a career on the East Coast, for that would keep pushing me past my comfort zone of my home, my roots, and what I knew.

So, when I found myself burned out working in a high-volume practice in Washington D.C., I knew I had to abandon that conventional path and build a practice that was 100 percent authentic to me. That meant ignoring everyone who said the "only way to be successful" is to spend thousands on running a practice, see patients every three minutes, and endure 12-hour days. I was miserable and fell into a two-year path that led to misery, weight gain, low self-esteem, and epic burnout.

This wasn't the type of doctor I wanted to be, so I spent the next six years building an unconventional practice with house calls. This allowed me to practice the way I wanted, work the way I wanted, and treat the way I wanted.

It was also the catalyst for me to realize that, in my heart of hearts, I am an entrepreneur. While I could have stayed comfortable in a thriving six-figure practice I was proud to have built, I knew my purpose was bigger and that I was supposed to shift my energy to mentoring others who were seeking unconventional ways to work and live like I was. To show them what was possible, that they're not alone, and that there is more out there for them.

So, I sold my practice, left what roots I had established in D.C., and moved to Miami to reinvent my work and my way of life. I struggled to find my identity and carve my path in running an online business, because my identity had been treating patients for the past eight years, after the regimen of academia. Like any new business owner, I had ebbs and flows. I had months where I had no idea how I was going to pay the rent and sometimes couldn't, but I knew it was what I was supposed to do. I knew that it was worth the risk to serve a bigger purpose. It was scary and exhilarating, and I questioned myself every step of the way.

Eventually I found my way and crawled out of the early stages to build a thriving online business, spending my days coaching and mentoring others on how to break away from the conventional practice model and say good-bye to burnout for good.

But despite my success in this area, I was miserable in Miami. I thrive in quiet, friendly communities, not ones filled with hustle and bustle. I tried to make a go of it, but after two years, I couldn't take the feeling of being a "fish out of water." Now the question was: "How do I find another place to try to call home?"

Then I realized that I didn't have to make that choice. Because of the decisions I made to have an online business, I had a newfound freedom, so I sold everything I owned and decided to become a "digital nomad," meaning I hopped from location to location, living anywhere and working from my laptop and smartphone.

Despite my newfound freedom and the success of my online business, I woke up 18 months into being a nomad realizing that something was missing.

I wasn't the person I told my nephew I wanted to be remembered for. On the surface, it looked great. I was loving the freedom of the lifestyle that allowed me more flexibility in my day-to-day than I ever had before.

I was able to pack my bags and fly home to be with family or friends at a moment's notice. I could create experiences by constantly living in and exploring new locations. For a girl like me who has wanderlust running through her veins, it was the perfect way of life.

So, you might be wondering, what could possibly be missing?

In the midst of all of this freedom, I found myself in my own trap. The same fears, insecurities, and doubts that I have had in my head for years remained with me.

I questioned myself on a regular basis. I doubted what I was capable of, and I was still creating boundaries within my own mind which, I grew to learn, is the ultimate thing that can hold all of us back in life.

Because that's what was happening to me.

What I really wanted was much deeper. I wanted a version of myself that was happier, leaner, more courageous, bolder, and more confident. Lifestyle aside, there were still goals I had put on hold. There were still adventures I was too afraid to try. There were still visions of the impact I could make and the greatness I felt within me that I still told myself I didn't deserve.

It was like a version of myself felt trapped inside and she was screaming at me to break free.

So, within my own lifestyle freedom, the irony was that I remained mired in yearning for a personal freedom that I hadn't fully created within my mind. I had built a mental prison in years of doubt and inhibition.

I realized that the only way to grow past what held me back was to hold myself accountable and in a big way. I was tired of putting deeper dreams on the back burner and created a challenge for myself based on this one question,

What if I could actually take action on the goals I had been putting on hold and make it all happen in 90 days?

How many ways can I serve and impact people around the world? How many ways can I give love and receive love? How many fears can I overcome? How many adventures can I experience? What things do I keep putting on hold because I'm telling myself I'm too scared, I'm not good enough, or it's *not the right time?*

Answering these questions and creating a 90-Day Life Challenge has become the cornerstone of what I do today and the impact I want to make.

This book is the culmination of the lessons and experiences that have brought me to where I am today, and the catalyst to answering these core questions:

1. Why are more people dissatisfied with their lives than ever before?

2. What causes people to feel stuck in life rather than thrive in it?

3. What are the behaviors, actions, and habits that can get people unstuck and create momentum in their lives?

4. How quickly can people change the course of their lives and the happiness they experience as a result?

My focus on these questions led me to mentor more than 5,000 students from around the world who have taken my online courses and various video trainings. I have had the opportunity to coach people out of burnout, away from jobs that left them unfulfilled, and through failing moments in their businesses, to create a new way of life based on what they truly want, not on what they thought they were "supposed to do."

I am honored to say that I have been named one of the Top 10 Wellness Leaders to Watch by Longevity Media, and my work has been featured in publications like *The Washingtonian* and *Modern Luxury Magazine* because of my innovative approach to creating more fulfillment in work and life.

This all happened because I took a stand for myself. I stopped listening to the noise and started to listen from within. I made a pact with myself to try to make sure no one feels stuck or trapped in their life, like I did in mine.

What This Book Is and Isn't

I want to be 100 percent honest with you. I have an agenda for writing this book. I have an agenda for you in reading it.

What my agenda is NOT is showing you how to become a digital nomad, traveler, online entrepreneur or leave your 9 to 5. While I am all of those things and happily so, that's not the point. It's what I've learned through this that cuts at a deeper motivation.

I am asking you to take a deeper look within yourself and find out what parts you've let go quiet, because you've told yourself that you're not good enough, you can't do it, or it's not the right time.

My agenda is simple. I want you to break away from the ways you've held yourself back. I want you to recognize that there is a greater, happier, more-fulfilled version of you waiting for you to take action so you can start creating your life and moving your dreams to the forefront.

I'm asking you to let go of the fears that have become a cycle and habit in your mind. I am asking you to be bold in what you want, to be open to any and all possibilities. And to embrace that part of this journey is to break you away from what the conventional life instructs you to do.

This is your time to chase the dream... not the fear, and to be brave to say "enough" and stop settling for the status quo.

There is no right time. You create your time. Life didn't just happen to you. You are in the driver's seat.

I broke away from what I was told I was "supposed to" do.

I was "supposed to" stay in one place and work in one location to build a practice and name for myself, rather than sell everything I owned.

I was "supposed to" be attached to one career because I spent $150,000 on student loans and eight years of my life studying how to do it, rather than become a self-taught entrepreneur and build an online business.

I was "supposed to" suck it up and stay in a place I didn't thrive in because I had a job and opportunities there, and after all, a job provides stability, right?

I was "supposed to" put success over happiness, rather than give myself the ability to realize I can actually have both at the same time.

I've already woken up several times in my life realizing I need to make a change before I hit the age of 40.

I've also learned that you can change the course and quality of your life quickly. I've learned that we are each capable of more in our lives than who we currently are. I've learned that 90 days can be all it takes to create a new version of yourself that is more fulfilled with life.

For the purpose of this book, I believe we crossed paths at this time because this is a message you need to hear. Somewhere within you, you've been searching for this kind of wake-up call.

You know you want to address the deeper issues that you've been afraid to face. You know you want to break away from your fears, self-defeating talk, limiting mindset, perfectionism, and all the other nonsense that has gotten in your way.

Most people never get to this place. Most people are too scared to face this, but you're not one of them. You are brave. You are determined, and you are hungry to break away from whatever ruts, traps, or routines block you from pure joy.

This is about a new journey from the day-to-day grind to creating daily happiness, a new you, a new way of life, and leveraging time in your favor.

90-Day Life Challenge

> *"Give me six hours to chop down a tree and I will spend the first four sharpening the axe."*

> — **ABRAHAM LINCOLN**

The most effective way to embark on changes in your life is to go into it with a well-executed plan. Together we are about to embark on a transformation, something so powerful that it merits planning and awareness to get the most out of it.

In order to help you create an effective 90-Day Life Challenge, I've broken down the book into three separate sections:

Section 1: Reflection

Section 2: Priorities and Planning

Section 3: Action

I know for some it may be tempting to just skip ahead to Section 3 and get right to work, but the work we do upfront together is what will help you get the most out of the journey you're about to begin.

To get the most out of creating a 90-Day Life Challenge in your life, you must understand first what brought you to this point. Why do you want to do this? How has your heart guided you here? Who are you currently and what is missing in your life?

Section 1 is all about helping you re-remember yourself and course-correct the direction of your life, because something is bringing you to this moment, this watershed. You need to understand what that is for you. And I will guide you through different arenas of your life to help you figure out what roadblocks got in your way and what dreams you have put on the back burner.

Knowing this will prepare you for Section 2: Priorities and Planning. This is an opportunity for you to lay new groundwork for your life, helping to establish a foundation for getting your own 90-Day Life Challenge into motion.

Then Section 3: Action is all structure. It's putting the plan to work and envisioning how to implement the 90-Day Life Challenge in your own life.

My goal for you is to discover by the end of your 90-Day Life Challenge a new version of yourself that puts fear to the side, takes action on goals, and builds amazing momentum for continued growth on your journey.

Along the way, I will guide you through self-reflective questions in each chapter that will elevate your level of awareness and understanding of how the message applies to you. I would highly recommend that you keep a journal dedicated to this book and these questions, so this becomes a very interactive experience for you.

There is something powerful in allowing your mind to freely think and write. It opens up a new creative space for you to be open to reflections and create an experience that is unique to you.

If you want to chart your discoveries in a guided, step-by-step way, go to **90daylifebook.com/workbook** to get my 90-Day Life Workbook, with sections devoted to each chapter and the lessons within.

If you're inspired and want to discover the quickest way to put the 90-Day Life Challenge into action in your life, watch this FREE VIDEO TRAINING, and say "YES" to rebuilding your life in 90 days:

90daylifebook.com/free-video-training

Section 1:

REFLECTION

Discover who you are now ...
and who you want to become.

CHAPTER 1:

WHY IMPERMANENCE WILL SET YOU FREE

"Yesterday is gone. Tomorrow has not yet come. We have only today. Let us begin."

— MOTHER TERESA

Time.

Some days we stare at the clock waiting for the day to be over, and other days we wish we could stop the clock altogether.

The clock always ticks, and it feels like time keeps moving faster.

There's nothing to time.

Days, weeks, and years feel faster the older we get. Our age surprises us no matter how many candles are on the birthday cake.

We live, breathe, and die by time. We look to the clock to tell us when we should eat, sleep, leave for work, go on a date, work out, and rest. From the time we set our alarm clock to wake up to the time we wait for our favorite show to start, our lives are controlled by time.

So much of our time is now scheduled out for us that our free time and how we spend it has become a precious resource.

After all, time keeps moving, whether we move with it or not. It never replenishes. We can replenish our food, our sleep, our energy, but we can never get back our time.

It's why the regrets of the dying all revolve around one core idea: "How did they spend their time?"

Or rather, how did they waste it?

Did they waste it on work that left them unfulfilled, in relationships where they were unhappy, in a state of anger and frustration?

Or did they spend it on meaningful work, unconditionally loving relationships, and joyous emotions?

How are you spending your time now?

People live by the clock but don't live into the time they are given.

If anything defines my purpose, it's teaching how to transform time into something that every single person should leverage, rather than wait for, or put off. The people who truly feel fulfilled in their lives are those who have mastered the art of leveraging their time.

They embrace it. They understand it. They aren't afraid to stare it in the face and soak up every minute of it. They plan how to spend it with precision and focus. They know why they do what they do and when they do it. They have mastered time.

This principle of leveraging time will be the cornerstone of rebuilding your life in 90 days, and it all starts with embracing impermanence. As your mentor, I will inspire you to redefine what time means to you, and how you spend it. You will learn the art of actually loving that the clock is always ticking, rather than feeling like there's never enough time.

The definition of impermanence is this: "Not lasting or durable; not permanent."

Nothing in life ever truly lasts. People come and go into our lives, as do jobs, homes, opportunities, and money. We can never repeat a moment in our past, no matter how many times we relive it in our mind. Once the moment is gone, it is gone forever, and nothing but a memory.

Life, in and of itself, is impermanent.

We all hope to grow old and live long lives, but no matter how old we are graced to be, at some point, our lives will end.

It is what we do with the time we are given that matters.

In front of you, right now, is a choice. You can choose to take time for granted. Or you can choose to make the most of it.

What I learned as a digital nomad is the power of impermanence when you choose it as a daily practice and as a way of life.

I get to experience mini-chapters of life that can range from living in the mountains one month to strolling along the beach the next, all while fitting everything that I need to work, live, and thrive in a suitcase.

With this, I realize that I have to make the most of my time, otherwise I will lose out while being in a destination. It takes nothing for days, weeks to go by and turn into the thought of "where has the time gone," which is the question that we all ask ourselves throughout life and even more so as we get older.

What's interesting about this lifestyle, though, is that I choose it. I choose how long I want to live in a certain place and experience a certain lifestyle.

I choose how much time I want to spend in one location, and I can choose whether to plan out a year of where I want to live, or spontaneously pick up and go.

With this lifestyle comes a challenge and an opportunity.

It's the same challenge and opportunity we all have, regardless of your lifestyle, how you live, or where you are living.

The challenge is how to be intentional with your time, so you feel complete with how you spend it and create a life where you can go to bed every night feeling complete in what you made of the day now behind you, rather than lament what you didn't do.

We take time for granted because we aren't forced to stare the clock in the face. When our time feels short, we would give anything to rewind the clock and do it over. When impermanence stares you in the face, like when faced with a diagnosis or when experiencing the sudden loss of a loved one, our perception of time changes.

It's why people who are blessed with second chances say their perspective on life has completely flipped. They no longer fill their time with things that don't make them happy, or things that distract them. They live without fear, with a renewed reckless abandon just to be and live. No questions, no doubts, no inhibitions.

Just purely living.

The opportunity in front of you is to do just that. To choose it and to know how to make it a way of life. To know what to do with your time and reassess how you are spending it, so you can make the most of it.

This opportunity creates the ultimate impermanence. You force yourself to live and enjoy every day because your days are numbered. We don't know how many days we have. We don't know whether today or tomorrow will be our last.

Impermanence symbolizes the clock that is ticking for all of us. I feel grateful and humbled to have learned this lesson at this stage of my life and even more grateful to be able to pass it on to you.

I should also share that I'm *not* interested in going in-depth into the nomadic chapter of my life. I want to extend the lessons from it, yes, but it is only a piece of the picture. I don't care what your specific way of life is. What I do care about is that you address this one question right now, rather than putting it off.

"Am I truly happy?"

Within that question lies a second one, "Am I truly happy with how I am spending my time?" Being able to say yes to both these questions is the key to a happy, fulfilled life. One that you can look back on at any moment and feel fulfilled.

Achieving this takes practice. It takes reinventing the way you approach every day of your life. It means stripping off the distractions and clutter and truly evaluating what you do in every moment.

People tend to avoid looking at their life this way because it can feel daunting on the surface. There is something that each and every one of us is putting on hold for a time in the future. And when a mirror of this truth gets reflected back at you, you can either run from it or face it.

Instinctively we fear time because the clock is ticking, but if we actually channel that fear into good, that is the starting point of making time work for you.

Imagine what it could feel like if you chose impermanence consciously, rather than because of circumstance. What would that feel like if you woke up every day with vigor and a zest for life? What if you walked into your job every day with a sense of purpose? What if you appreciated the people in your life and lived with gratitude and contentment?

What if you created moments of spontaneity in your life while, along the way, loving the routines you do have?

What if you chose to live your life every day like it was your last?

The only thing that defines how you view your life and the time you're given is the choice you make. Don't fear the clock. Instead, embrace it. Don't wish for weekends or vacations. Instead, fall in love with Mondays again.

Live your life every day so it feels like a vacation because you choose to love what you are doing, whatever you are doing, every single moment.

As your mentor, I will inspire you to look at time in a whole new way and show you how you can change the course of, and happiness in, your life much faster than you have ever realized. You will learn a step-by-step process to re-evaluate your life and take a stand for what you really want, and go after it. I will show you that time is actually your best friend, your motivator, and your partner in this crazy journey called life.

If you allow yourself to be vulnerable in this journey and be open to the reflections you are gaining as you go through this book, I have full confidence that the next 90 days can completely transform your life.

How I Lived More in 90 Days Than in Seven Years

I spent seven years of my life living in Washington, D.C.

I wanted to visit every Smithsonian museum, but only got to visit two. I wanted to pursue rowing on the Potomac, but I let my insecurities about the water, my weight, and physical fitness get in the way, despite being told by former rowing coaches that I'd be perfect for the sport. There were restaurants and historic sites I wanted to visit that I never got to because I thought, "I'll get to it later."

But I never did.

The same cycle of putting things off happened in Miami Beach, until I was three months away from leaving. I was so focused on wanting to move away from a city where I didn't fit that I forgot to enjoy it along the way. I woke up and realized that I only had a little bit of time left, and I better get cracking on all the things I wanted to do while there was still time.

The clock was ticking, and the urgency to live kicked back on.

So, I started every day watching the sun rise on the beach. I swam in the pool every day. I took up rowing and got to experience first-hand the crystal blue waters of Biscayne Bay. My coach said I was a natural and thought I was one of her veteran rowers in the boat.

In that instant, I felt the pain of regret. I saw the flash of years I wasted getting stuck in my own head and not pursuing something I knew I would truly love.

But I also felt the catalyst of motivation to not live with regrets again.

I had lived more in 90 days than I had in seven years.

All because I heard the clock ticking. This made me appreciate my surroundings, the opportunities there, and the activities that gave me joy.

That taste of impermanence gave me a taste of freedom, and that was a gift, a gift I now want to pass on to you.

Impermanence Creates Action

It's easy to forget what's important and what you want to spend your time doing. It's easy to take our lives, loved ones, and surroundings for granted because it's easier to think that they'll always be there than to realize that, someday, they'll be gone. It's easy to get lost in the day-to-day life of routines, distractions, crazy schedules, and endless to-dos. It's easy to tell yourself, "I don't have time for it," or "I'll get to that later."

But what if you don't have the time?

How do you know if you'll *ever* have the time?

You don't. None of us does.

The power of impermanence is that it creates urgency to live, to love, and to make a difference. When you have a sense of urgency, you take action. When you take action, you create momentum. When you have momentum, you experience a new level of growth and happiness in your life.

Impermanence gives you the freedom to:

- Not get lost in your fears.
- Break away from your doubts.
- Act without inhibition.

The power in choosing impermanence is that you have a renewed sense of how you spend your life, rather than waiting for life to happen. In our journey together, you'll get to choose how you want to live out the next 90 days.

That doesn't mean you have to do something radical, but it does mean is that you must snap out of mindless routines and wake up your life and your desires again.

In fact, you could make absolutely no changes in your life. You could wake up on day 90 doing exactly the same thing you were on day 1. But you would have created an opportunity to reconsider all of your choices, fully assess the merits of each against all the possibilities, and then chosen purposefully to do all of those things anyway.

Unlikely, but this would be a mindful choice, and maybe liberating because you will have a renewed appreciation for the life you have and what you have created for yourself.

That's the power of impermanence. You feel liberated because it spurs action with the clock, rather than against it.

This is now your opportunity to remember the things you've been wanting to do and have been putting off, whether that's from excuses, fears, stresses, or any thoughts or circumstances you've allowed to hold you back.

All because you are now making the choice to put time on your side.

That's the opportunity that we have in front of us, and that's what I hope to bring into your life — a new zest drawn from urgency and living in the here and now.

To begin making impermanence a habit, you have to reflect on these three questions:

1. What are the things in your life you have been taking for granted because they are always there?

2. What have you been putting off in life because you tell yourself "I'll get to it later," even though it's something that's important to you and what you want to do?

3. How would your life be different if you acted like today was your last?"

Because those are the things that you now have the ability to bring into your life and stop putting on the back burner.

These things in your life can be anything from your loved ones, your health, your prosperity, your surroundings, or your material things.

They can also be the things that you have been wanting to have, do, create, or achieve that you have been putting on hold.

In the next three chapters, we'll address how to put impermanence into deeper practice by evaluating where you currently are in life and looking into the future, so you never take time for granted again.

CHAPTER 2:

MAPPING CHOICES

"The choices we make lead up to actual experiences. It is one thing to decide to climb a mountain. It is quite another to be on top of it."

— **HERBERT A. SIMON**

KEITH IS ON the phone with me, in a fit of tears, and confesses: "I feel like a complete failure."

On the surface, you would see an engaging, fit, charismatic 30-something, who loved life and loved adventure. When not at work, Keith had a passion for adrenaline rushes in the outdoors like cliff-diving. He wasn't afraid to take risks and was eager to be great. Newly married, starting a young family, and in the beginnings of his career, it appeared he had his whole life in front of him.

But Keith felt like everything had stopped in its tracks. He was three years into a career that he anticipated to be a path of promise, potential, and making a difference. He was certain that he would never have to question his ability to provide for his family or question his level of satisfaction in his work. He had dreams of being able to give his wife the chance to quit her job, so she could focus on her own business. He envisioned being able to set aside money for college for his children.

Where he ended up, though, was quite different. His current job had him working 60 hours a week, rushing through his client appointments, and only making a fraction of what he brought into the business. His bank account was meager, and he was scraping to get by every month. His wife ended up working more hours to pay the bills, meanwhile they had to put off family vacations because the money was just too tight.

He was at a tipping point. Something needed to change and change very quickly.

As a coach, I honor and value the trust that my clients give me. It's a vulnerable journey getting coached, and the people I attract are those who are hungry for change and an accountability partner to elevate their life to the next level. It's my responsibility to push people to work through what is holding them back, and sometimes that unleashes a wellspring of buried emotions and frustrations.

It's in moments like these, when a client is breaking down on the phone, that I make sure to create a safe space where they can express without judgment, because it's in those moments where a breakthrough is ready to emerge.

As I hear his tears on the other end of the line, I knew I had to both challenge and comfort Keith, so I did what I do often in this situation, I help my clients find clarity.

"Keith, what does failure mean to you?" I asked.

"I feel so stuck and lost. I never thought I would be broke or hate my job or not be able to take care of my family. This isn't what I wanted. This isn't how I saw my career going," he replied.

I knew I had to keep going deeper. Sometimes in moments of failure, we feel so completely lost that we forget what we really want and who we really are. It's not my job to tell my clients what that is; it's my job to help them rediscover it or maybe find it for the first time ever.

I knew Keith had his clarity somewhere deep inside of him, so I asked him, "How did you see your career going?"

His voice quickened and he started to speak faster, like he realized all along who he had been saying no to for the past three years.

"I've always wanted to have my own business. Before I graduated, I already knew how I wanted to be different from a typical business in my field. So many of my peers care about volume and money, rather than the quality of their work. I wanted to provide more care and attention to my clients rather than treat them all the same. I wanted to have the freedom to set my own fees and hours, so I could have the flexibility to spend more time with my family and in the outdoors. I wanted something I could call my own."

This wasn't the version of Keith that existed now. In fact, it was quite the opposite. How did Keith wake up to something so completely different from what he wanted?

That's why I kept prodding. I had to get him to understand how he had held himself back and what choices took him off the path he really wanted.

"Why didn't you just start own business after graduating then?"

His tone starts to change. He starts to sound more frustrated and aware at the same time.

"Well everyone in school told me that I should work for someone else first. That I would need some experience before I knew what it would take to start my own business.

My professors and friends kept telling me to start off the first few years in a job, save up, build a nest egg, and then I can do my own thing. I never really wanted to do it, but I thought it made the most sense and it's what everyone was telling me to do."

This was really the crux of Keith's feeling of failure. It's not that he fell short of his vision because he was working too many hours or wasn't making the money he wanted.

It's that he had failed himself. He stopped listening to what he knew he wanted and instead focused on what other people thought was best for him.

He was living a life of "should."

He forgot who he was at a pivotal point in his life and that took him off the path he really wanted. This wasn't the true, convicted, adventure-loving Keith. This was the housebroken, socially domesticated, follow-the-pack version of Keith, which really wasn't Keith at all.

I had to help him find the real Keith again. So, I paused for a moment and let his answer linger. I wanted him to feel the discomfort of his realization before asking him something which initially seemed completely off topic, "Why do you love cliff-diving?"

"It's the best feeling in the world. I can just let go. I don't think about it because if I do, I won't do it. I love the adrenaline right before I start running towards the edge and the freedom of just letting go once my feet hit the air and I freefall. I feel nothing, and I feel everything in a flash. I feel free."

"Then it sounds like it's time to bring out that adrenaline junkie, Keith, and just dive."

I'm guessing you know someone like Keith in your life, or maybe you've been in his shoes, where you woke up to a life that was based on what you were told to do or supposed to do, as opposed to what you really want.

Keith was living the life he was because he was listening to everything he thought he "should" do, rather than acting on what he knew he could do.

Where you are in your life right now is the direct result of the choices you've made before this very moment. You are the consequence of your choices, good or bad, and every choice you make will either take you on a path toward who you really are or take you away from it.

One set of choices leads to life burnout; the other leads to life fulfillment.

A path of choices based on "should" feels safe and easy, because we don't have to think about them. They are placed in front of us and we feel validated by other people encouraging us that this is what is best for our life.

But there's no adrenaline in that. There's no joy. The comfort from this path is only based on not looking fear in the face and going for what you want, regardless of how many "shoulds" come your way.

What would your life feel like if you just dove in and went for it? What if you stopped listening to the noise, the opinions, the naysayers, and listened to yourself again?

Bucking the Status Quo

Just because society has a definition of what typical day-to-day life looks like doesn't mean you have to live it.

If your life is the direct result of what other people think is best for you, life will just happen to you. That's the status quo. Follow the leader. Say yes. Keep your head down. Don't ask questions, and just do what you're told. Play the percentages.

It's a comfortable life. A life that doesn't involve awareness, growth, or courage, because it's a path already carved. It feels safe because it's also the path of others, and that's comforting to us as individuals. Following a trail is much easier than carving your own.

But just because the path is laid out for you doesn't mean that it's the path you're destined to travel. Each of us has unique gifts and talents that we can give back to the world to create an incredible life, and it's the choices you make that will either help or hinder your ability to express them.

As a kid, I grew up loving the Indiana Jones movies. If you're not familiar, Indiana Jones, played by the actor Harrison Ford, was an archaeologist and explorer who set out to find the world's most hidden and treasured artifacts. His adventures would lead to exotic locations all around the world and oftentimes off the beaten path. As he traveled, the movie would cut away from a scene of him to a scene of a world map with dots and lines charting his journey, so it felt like you were traveling with him.

I was always enamored by these scenes and how they mapped his journey from where he had been to where he was destined to land. You could immerse yourself in his world and see his path, because you were traveling on it with him. Each time he decided to pursue a new discovery, it would take him to a new location, and the map would expand into more dots and lines spanning the globe.

Before he traveled to a location, he had to make choices to get there, and every location was a tipping point. It was the location of a new chapter in his adventures. His decisions led him to the next flight, car ride, chase, and discovery.

We are all on our own adventure. We all have the opportunity to evaluate our choices and the destination, as well as change them in an instant.

As you look at your life, each pivotal moment was created by a choice. For example:

- Where you went to school.
- The job you accepted.
- Who you married.
- Where you live.

There was a culmination of decisions that led you to make the choice you did. Insert dot on the map. And that choice led to the next destination and milestone in your life. Draw line to next life chapter.

We always make the choices that feel best in that moment. Never do we intend to make a choice that we inherently know will be bad for us, but the question really is: "Where did this choice originate and has it brought you to the destination you want to reach?"

Mapping out your choices doesn't mean you should change or reverse the choices you have made. It's about understanding what choices have supported your path in life, and those that have taken you off of it.

Stop Tolerating Mediocre

It's difficult to look at your choices through this lens, because after all, they are yours. We get attached to the choices we have made because we have invested something in that choice, and we become more attached to it the longer we stick with it.

But the only thing your attachments will do to the choices that aren't serving you now is make you feel trapped by them. Accepting those choices as your unchangeable fate only strips away your power today and robs you of your happiness potential. It leads to a life that is mediocre. You feel ok. You're kind of happy. You've settled in life, and you're ok with that because you've grown used to it. You've let the choices of your past dictate what you do today, and your ability to change your life for tomorrow.

Keith could have chosen to tolerate mediocre for the rest of his life. He could have settled for his job, even though it was sucking the life out of him, because at least it provided some sense of stability. He and his wife could have struggled financially for years as a result and lived under the paradigm of, "no matter how hard we work, we'll just have to scrape by," then passed that lesson onto their children. Keith could have become the consequence of his choices and slowly let the aspirations of his youth fade away and get buried by doubt, acceptance, and tolerance.

But he didn't. His tolerance hit a breaking point. He could have either continued to play victim to it or finally said "enough." Think about how different his life would have been had he keep accepting mediocre.

Instead, Keith took a bet on himself. He began to trust that he had the knowledge to launch and build a successful business on his terms. Most important, he had a renewed desire for what he wanted and a determination to not settle.

And he did it. Just 18 months after his life wake-up call, Keith not only had a successful business, but he was able to provide for his family, give his wife the financial support to work on her own business, *and have more time for cliff-diving.*

You have a new choice in front of you right now, and that's the choice to stop tolerating mediocre. You deserve to have a life where you feel vibrant, alive, and joyful. You have the ability to evaluate your choices, which ones have served you, and which ones need course-correction.

You may have noticed that nowhere am I saying that your choices are right or wrong. They purely point you in a direction and you can glean lessons from them regardless of the direction they've taken you.

The key is what you do with the lessons you're learning.

What choices have you made to get you to where you are right now? Are you happy with your choices? Are you where you want to be? Is this the place you hoped to be in your life right now?

What choices have steered you off course and made you feel mediocre?

Understanding this will spark a renewed thirst to take a risk and bet on yourself. It's my job to help guide you to it, and it's your opportunity to discover it.

If you want to break away from the mediocrity and create a new set of choices that will better serve you, you must evaluate your choices and the level of satisfaction in each of these four areas of your life:

- #1 Your Health
- #2 Your Relationships
- #3 Your Contribution
- #4 Your Personal Growth

If you were to rank yourself on a scale from 0-10, with 0 meaning "no satisfaction" to 10 meaning "completely satisfied," how would you score yourself? Take a moment and write down your score for each, because this will be your baseline scores on Day 1, so you can reassess your growth on Day 90 of your challenge.

While there are several facets to a fulfilling life, your core transformation can be condensed into these four areas. If you want to have a successful 90-Day Life Challenge and truly elevate your life to a new level, you have to consider the following:

Your Health. We start with health because it is our most important asset, even more important than our time. With our health, we can do everything we want and we often take our health for granted. When we don't have good health, we would give anything to go back to a time when we did. What choices have led you to the level of health you have right now? Are you as healthy as you want to be or were at a younger age, or have you let your health slide? What choices have you made that have created your level of health right now?

Your Relationships: Are you surrounded by an inner circle of people in your life (your partner, family, and friends) that completely nourishes you, supports you, unconditionally loves you, inspires you, and allows you to be truly authentic? Or are you surrounding yourself with relationships that dis-empower you, that steal your joy and energy, or dampen your spirits? What choices have you made to have these people in your life right now?

Your Contribution. Does your work truly fulfill you? Do you feel like you are making an impact and contribution to the world and doing so in a way that taps into your core strengths? Or are you just working for the sake of having a job or getting a paycheck, and ignoring the very gifts and skills you have? What choices have you made to be contributing at this level during this current stage of your life?

Your Personal Growth. Are you constantly evolving in your goals, dreams, and aspirations? Do you challenge yourself on a consistent basis? Are you a consummate learner and fueling your brain and body with new habits and activities that bring you joy? Or are you the same person and in the same place you were five years ago? Are you filling your free time with distractions like TV and social media that really don't do anything good for you at all except fill your brain with chatter? What choices have you made in your personal growth? Are they helping you grow or stay stagnant?

You may be sensing that you have room for improvement in each of these areas. If you do, that's good news, because you'll start to get hungry for change. You aren't ranking yourself with 10s across the board because somewhere you have allowed yourself to accept choices that have not served you best.

Recognize the fact that you are in this place right now because something in you is craving change. If you're not ranking yourself with a 10 in each of these four areas, it's because you are holding yourself back from being fully satisfied. Look at each area and ask yourself: "What am I leaving on the table? Why do I feel dissatisfied? What needs to be unleashed inside of me that I have let go quiet?"

You will notice that there are choices and elements in your daily routine that serve you and others that need to be revamped.

Discovering this takes strength, courage, and clarity. You possess all of these qualities because you are here right now. Take a moment to honor that.

Because recognizing the power that is within you, in this moment, to look at yourself and your life gives you the foundation to create beautiful change.

Creating your life does not come from sticking with the status quo you have built.

Rather, it comes from breaking away from that feeling of mediocre and having a strategy to create instant changes and long-term transformations in your life.

There is a common thread in what mapping your choices means for all of us, and it is this:

What could your life look like if your past choices didn't hold you back anymore?

How much happier would you feel? How much freer would you feel?

This can be a powerful moment. Be gentle with yourself as you realize what has been holding you back. This is not about self-punishment or regret; just identification of choices to re-address for today and tomorrow.

The first step to change is discovery. This section of our journey together is where we get to reconnect with who you really are. Discovery will set you up for movement and action to bring more fulfillment into your life. It's a process that many people do not face, because it brings a lot out from under the surface.

What to Do Next

Map out your choices and rate yourself in each of the four areas: health, relationships, contribution, and personal growth. What choices have served you and what choices are holding you back?

Are there past choices that now, as you reflect on them, bring up resentment, fear, or frustration? Take note of both ends of the spectrum. Listen to what your heart is telling you in this question. You will find clarity in your choices here.

This realization is pivotal at this stage of your journey. The first step to change is awareness. Once you are aware of your choices, you can own your choices, and change your choices for the future.

In the next two chapters of this section, we'll address how to take control of your choices so they accelerate your growth and fulfillment in life.

CHAPTER 3:

OWNING YOUR CONSEQUENCES

*"The consequences of an act affect the
probability of its occurring again."*

— B. F. SKINNER

IT'S TIME TO look at your choices for what they are. A dot on
the map, nothing more, nothing less. Each choice leads to a
domino effect of what you will experience in your life. Each
choice will take you to a different destination.

I recognize that I'm asking you to look into your life and
evaluate it in a vulnerable, deep way right out of the gate.

If you feel anything like resistance, frustration, sadness, or
even a rude-awakening inside of you, this is a good thing.
It's a sign that you're recognizing you want something
more in your life. That is a recognition that too many don't
give themselves the opportunity to see. By recognizing
this now, though, you can avoid potential regrets later on
in life.

The awareness you're building right now is the secret
sauce to helping you break out of your rut. The key
however is to use that awareness to propel action, and not

hold onto those emotions or beat yourself up because of some of the decisions you have made. It's ok if you don't "get it all right." You won't. None of us will.

But what separates the people who lead an exquisite life from those who lead a mediocre life are those looks in the mirror on a regular basis to re-evaluate their life, ask the tough questions, and use their answers to create change.

Every choice has consequences, be they positive or negative. And it's linear, just like time.

Choice Leads to Consequence

It really is that simple.

Once you recognize this, you won't let emotions that well up as you reflect on your past get away with you. You can't change the past. You can't change what happened to you as a result of your past, so why beat yourself up over it? Emotions are just energy. You can either let that energy consume you or you can harness it to create good.

What you can change... is NOW.

Unfortunately, in today's age, we are driven by success, status, wealth, attention, and validation more than ever. There are more social pressures for perfection in magazines and social media with images of people who just seem to "have it all together," so it leads to an unrealistic expectation that we must get it all right, all the time, every time.

What we *are not* chasing here is perfection. We are not going to go on a hunt to get it all right, but we are going to look at your life in a more systematized, structured, reflective way where you can accept your choices, acknowledge your emotions, and then move on and not waste another moment on them, *so you can own the consequences of your choices now and chart a new path.*

Why the Mid-Life Crisis Happens

In Western society, there is a stigma. No, I'll go so bold to say that there is an expectation, that you will wake up somewhere in the middle of your life with a "what the heck am I doing?" moment. You will bottom out with a feeling that you have wasted time and will wake up to the regret of years and youth gone by.

People are shown to believe that the best way to cope with this moment is to react and make a spiral of rash decisions to try to reclaim the happiness and youth forgone.

This period is stereotypically portrayed with images of men seeing the first silver streaks in their hair going out to buy a convertible to feel young again, or women seeking invasive ways to remove the signs of aging from their faces and bodies to bring back their glow as a 20-year-old.

The midlife crisis carries a negative stigma. It symbolizes dreams we've put to the wayside or a version of ourselves that is long gone, leaving us feeling empty, unfulfilled, and primed to make rash decisions to turn it all around.

On the flip side, when we reach the middle period of our lives, we also must deal with a societal belief that this is when we should have our act together. The career, the paycheck, the house, the kids, the IRA, and the car.

So, it's no wonder that when people reach a crossroads in their life, no matter at what age, it's challenging to face and even harder to share.

We don't want to be seen as a failure in the eyes of our family, friends, co-workers, society, or ourselves.

And if we find ourselves not being "middle age," then it's even worse when we find ourselves in a place in our lives where we're not happy, because that is not what is expected of us.

So not only does the conventional path get laid out for you, it can set you up for failure or resentment down the road. We have forgotten to allow ourselves to be vulnerable, to be reflective, and to seek change at any age.

We aren't taught that it is natural or actually healthy to constantly evolve and grow in life. It's not what the hamster wheel of convention is teaching us, so we stay stuck in a conventional routine and that's why we wake up to a life we don't want. We aren't taught the power of owning the consequences of our choices, and how to channel our displeasure with them into motivation going forward. Rather, we let them dis-empower us.

The Quarter-Life Crisis is Now a Thing

With our lifespans getting longer on average with each generation, the period where we're expected to be on the conventional path and stay on it is getting longer, which is why millennials are in for a "worse mid-life crisis" than their parents.[3]

In fact, the "quarter-life crisis" is now the new mid-life crisis. More people in their 20s are waking up to that "what the heck" life moment than ever before. Rising college costs, high job expectations, societal pressures, and our current culture of "more is better" is the perfect storm for a rude awakening to a life they didn't expect once they start their career. It sets the path for disappointment.

The bottom line here is that we have lost our power.

We have put our happiness in the hands of things that we believe to be outside of our control, like our circumstances, the beliefs of others, and what society is telling us about how to live.

You can't control what others think is best for you or their opinions of you. What you can control, however, are your choices, and the consequences that result.

If the choices we've made to get us where we are today haven't led to the results we expected, it's getting easier to play the blame game on things outside of ourselves rather than ask: "What can I do to change my life right now?"

If you can own that the consequences you are experiencing have come from your choices, you are now harnessing the ability to change those consequences from within. The decision process that got you to this point can also get you out of it, no matter what area of your life you are looking to improve.

Monica was in the thick of a perfect storm. She was eight years into a marriage that had been suffering for some time, though she was afraid to admit it. She and her husband had a beautiful, happy 3-year-old boy who was the bond that kept them together. She felt that they were great parents, but they weren't great partners. They co-existed every day and worked together great as a team, but they were slowly growing apart. It was an elephant in the room of their home that was taking up more space by the day, but Monica was at a loss for how to look it in the eye and confront it.

What made matters worse was that she had just completed graduate school, which her husband had financially supported her through. Now she was on the brink of starting her own business, which her husband was also financially backing, all while balancing the responsibilities of raising her son. She loved being a mother, but felt like she was losing a part of herself along the way. What she really felt was trapped. Trapped by a relationship of obligation. Trapped by a relationship of attachment and the financial support her husband was providing. Trapped by eight years of history and memories they had built within their home.

Within that trap was a sad, disheartened Monica. She no longer felt nourished in her relationship. She and her husband had been growing apart for some time, and she felt they were no longer the partners they used to be.

In our initial coaching call, what she openly admitted to me was, "I deserve better, but I'm afraid to ask myself for it."

You can imagine how delicate of a situation this was for me to coach her during this period of her life.

Important Side Note: I am not a psychologist, psychiatrist, counselor or consultant, nor is it my job to tell people what to do or what life decisions to make or change. I do my best work with people who feel stuck on a conventional path, whatever convention means for them. I get paid to help people find out for themselves what it is they want in life, and act on it, rather than be afraid of it.

It was not my job to tell Monica what to do with her marriage or her business. It was my responsibility to help her discover the truth within herself and use that to set the course for the next stage in her life.

In the end, what everyone has the right to experience in life is the right to be happy and fulfilled. The right to have a freedom of choice, to not let the consequences of their life trap them, and to change their life in an instant. The clients I attract feel trapped in some way, and whether that's through their perspective or through their consequences, I help them break out of the box they have built around themselves and start to own their consequences, so they can act differently.

Monica was in the thick of her own "mid-life crisis." She woke up to the consequences of being in a failing marriage and dependent on people outside of herself for stability.

She lost her power. She lost her sense of self-reliance. She forgot to trust in herself.

We needed to rebuild that again. She needed to see that she can own the consequences of every choice she has made, both in what is nourishing her as well as dis-empowering her.

She needed to see that there is a difference between owning her consequences as opposed to being attached to them and feeling like she needs to just settle for life as it is. I knew that would take a huge dose of courage. All change does, but I also knew that if I could show her that difference, then she would see that where she is in her life right now is actually a gift and a catalyst to something better.

The Mid-Life Christmas

There is a classic U-shaped curve of happiness[4] that has been shown by research to be universal across various countries and cultures.

This shows that happiness steadily increases through the middle period of life, then gradually decreases as we get older.

I find these results troubling. It paints a reality that so many people face, expect, and, even worse, experience.

I believe we have the power to actually change that, rather than expect it. I believe if we stop listening to what we're being told to expect from life, we can steadily grow into more happiness over time, as opposed to expect that it will drop off once we reach that false notion of "over the hill."

I believe that the secret to doing this is by harnessing the power and potential within us to create whatever we want, whenever we want, and believe that it is possible.

I believe in flipping the conventional myth that a mid-, quarter-, anytime-life crisis exists, and actually think of it as a "Mid-Life Christmas."

If you can own the consequences of your choices, like Monica was beginning to discover, you can create a self-reliance to trust in yourself again. You can also start to see that in every consequence, there is a lesson to be learned, and that you have the ability to harness that lesson for positive change. You can use it as fuel to see that the version of you right now wants more, deserves more, and demands more.

Monica was in a relationship that wasn't nourishing her. The negative consequences of that were the strife, stress, and struggles between her and her husband. What she didn't see prior to coaching were the positive consequences of her choices as well. Once she did, she stopped feeling like a victim and started to become the architect. Because of where she was in her life, she started to realize that she deserved more. She deserved a partner who could support her on every level, not just from a financial standpoint. She wanted a partner who was her friend, confidant, lover, and inspiration.

Monica was also a proud mother. She adored her son and would do anything for him. The positive consequence of being a parent was the sense of pride, purpose, and unconditional love that she had in her life and could give to her son. On the negative side, she felt attached to staying in her marriage because of it.

She was boxing herself in rather than seeing the paths in front of her, and realizing that she could break out of the box or re-create it any time she wanted to.

My goal was to show Monica that every choice has consequences and oftentimes, the consequences have pros and cons. I knew that once she realized this, she would be able to own those consequences, rather than feel trapped by them, and use this as a catalyst to not only make choices that would support the future direction of her life, but that she could better weigh the consequences of each decision to help her get on a path where she felt more authentic, alive, and free.

This means you can look at the current stage of your life, no matter what your age, and do a deep cleanse of thoughts, decisions, habits, and choices that aren't serving you, so you can step into the dreams and goals you've been wanting to go after. There are one of two ways this can go:

1. If you aren't happy with something in your life right now, you can change your perspective to realize that the positive consequences are greater than the negative.

2. If the negative outweighs the positive, you can make choices to change your current life circumstances to produce a better result.

For Monica, she realized it was #2. She had put in a valiant effort to make her marriage and current way of life work, and she was at peace with that. This gave her the confidence to end her relationship, despite her fears of going out on her own, because she knew it would lead to more freedom and happiness. Was she terrified? Absolutely. But she was at a point in her life where she wasn't going to let her fears get the best of her.

> *"Even the bravest have fears, but it is not enough to stop them from moving in the path they are destined to walk upon."*
>
> **— ANONYMOUS**

Let's revisit the choices you mapped out in the previous chapter. Now look at those choices again, especially the ones you've discovered aren't serving you, and ask yourself, "what are the consequences of these choices that I'm experiencing today?" Then ask yourself, "what are the positive lessons from these consequences that I can use to make new choices in my life?"

Once you understand what those life lessons are, you can look at each of those lessons and determine a choice you can make as a result. This will create the framework for what you want to make happen in the next 90 days.

We'll address this more in-depth in the upcoming chapters, where we look at reshaping your inner beliefs and prioritizing what's important to you, so you know what to take action on and how to believe in yourself again.

This is an opportunity. You are here reading this for a reason. Because you are looking to change. You know you want to change. And you are taking action toward doing just that.

Throughout this section of the book, we are creating a foundation for your 90-Day Life Challenge to help you find your power again, so you know how to create a new version of yourself step-by-step.

It's a chance to wake yourself up and really look at what makes you happy, and to recognize what choices will take you on the path you want, rather than the path you or others think you should follow.

This brings me to one of my favorite stories that I'd like to share. It's a short story on life and living and how creating the life you want can be simpler that you think.

What We Can Learn from the Mexican Fisherman

An American investment banker was at the pier of a small coastal Mexican village when a small boat with just one fisherman docked. Inside the small boat were several large yellow fin tuna. The American complimented the Mexican on the quality of his fish and asked how long it took to catch them.

The Mexican replied, "only a little while." The American then asked why didn't he stay out longer and catch more fish? The Mexican said he had enough to support his family's immediate needs. The American then asked, "but what do you do with the rest of your time?"

The Mexican fisherman said, "I sleep late, fish a little, play with my children, take siestas with my wife, Maria, stroll into the village each evening where I sip wine, and play guitar with my amigos. I have a full and busy life."

The American scoffed, "I am a Harvard MBA and could help you. You should spend more time fishing and with the proceeds, buy a bigger boat. With the proceeds from the bigger boat, you could buy several boats, eventually you would have a fleet of fishing boats. Instead of selling your catch to the middleman you would sell directly to the processor, eventually opening your own cannery. You would control the product, processing, and distribution. You would need to leave this small coastal fishing village and move to Mexico City, then LA and eventually New York City, where you will run your expanding enterprise."

The Mexican fisherman asked, "But, how long will this all take?"

To which the American replied, "15-20 years."

"But what then?" asked the Mexican.

The American laughed and said, "That's the best part. When the time is right, you would announce an IPO and sell your company stock to the public and become very rich, you would make millions!"

"Millions – then what?"

The American said, "Then you would retire. Move to a small coastal fishing village where you would sleep late, fish a little, play with your kids, take siestas with your wife, stroll to the village in the evenings where you could sip wine and play your guitar with your amigos."

If you spend your life attached to choices based on what others think or on what you decided in the past, you will wake up to a life you don't want.

Owning your consequences is what will give you the ability to avoid the "mid-life crisis" all together, or if you're in the thick of one, you can now look at it as a gift.

No longer will the authentic side of you feel buried. You'll stop feeling like your dreams are too far in the distance, and you'll stop believing the conventional story that to live a fulfilling life you have to settle for less, work hard and hope the rewards will come, and wait it out for a while.

When you create choices that are in better alignment with what you really want, the rewards will come faster and you will feel more satisfied along the journey, rather than waiting for the satisfaction to come when time gets around to delivering it.

Where the Mexican fisherman is wise beyond what society or the conventional path of life is telling us, to wit: You can have your life right now. You can live it right now. If you focus on the priorities that are the most important to you, that will make an instant switch in the quality of your life.

It will give you the power to actually create a "Mid-Life Christmas" for yourself, no matter what stage of life you occupy. Because this journey truly is a gift to wake up and recognize that there is more within you that you want to bring out into the light.

Before You Go to the Next Chapter...

Revisit the choices you mapped out in the previous chapter.

Now look at those choices again, one by one, especially the ones that you've discovered aren't serving you, and ask yourself these two questions:

1. What are the consequences of these choices that I'm experiencing today? List them out next to each choice and then put a "+" next to each positive consequence and a "-" next to each negative consequence.

2. Then ask yourself, what are the positive lessons from these consequences that I can use to make new choices in my life?

CHAPTER 4:

PREDICTING REGRETS

"Twenty years from now, you will be more disappointed by the things you didn't do than by the ones you did do. So throw off the bowlines. Sail away from the safe harbor. Catch the trade winds in your sails. Explore. Dream. Discover."

— MARK TWAIN

AT THE END of our lives, I believe we all want the same thing. We want to look back and know that we took the time to focus on the important things, time with our loved ones, and doing the things we enjoy. We want to look back and be happy with the person we were, because we never said no to ourselves. We lived into who we really were without doubt or question. We want to know that we had courage. We lived with a fearless abandon to soak up every moment.

You don't want to look back on your life wishing you had worked more, made more, hated more, or guessed more. You don't want to look back and wish you had let fear run your life. You don't want to look back and wish you had let others dictate your happiness rather than find it within yourself.

But we end up spending huge portions of our lives not living into what we want because we have held ourselves back in some way. Whether in our mind, from things outside of us, or a combination of both, people typically end up looking back on their lives wishing they would have done things differently.

This chapter is about harnessing the power to predict the regrets in your life. It's about how you can look forward and anticipate what you could be missing out on and how to act on those things now, while you can, rather than putting them off. Regrets don't have to be an absolute in your life. They don't have to be something that you should expect or anticipate having just because others have experienced it.

Whether you have regrets already or will in later stages of your life comes down to two things:

The first revolves around what you do with the time you are given.

Bronnie Ware, a palliative nurse and speaker, wrote a best-selling memoir "The Top Five Regrets of the Dying: A Life Transformed by the Dearly Departing"[5] based on her observations and personal experiences. She determined that these regrets are:

1. I wish I had the courage to live a life true to myself, not the life others expected of me.

2. I wish I hadn't worked so hard.

3. I wish I had the courage to express my feelings.

4. I wish I had stayed in touch with my friends.

5. I wish I had let myself be happier.

Of those five regrets, #1 was reported as the most common. What Bronnie discovered is that people who lived based on what others expected of them ended up doing things they didn't want to do and spent too much of their lives doing them. They lived a life of fear and complacency. They said "yes" to everyone else, but said "no" to themselves.

This sets the course of what you do versus what you don't do.

If you choose courage, you will act on the things you want, regardless of what anyone thinks, because you know it is right for you.

In your 90-Day Life Challenge, I will teach you how to create a bucket list. We're not going to create an endless list of all the things that you want to do in life. In my experience, that can create a sense of longing and overwhelm from questioning whether everything on that list can get scratched off before our time is up.

I'm not going to set that expectation for you. It creates too big of a gap between where you are now and what you want to achieve in your life. It's also the reason why most New Year's resolutions fail in just a few weeks. People set too lofty of goals without a clear road on how to accomplish them, and don't break them down into smaller benchmarks they can achieve in the near future. So, it's easier to give up shortly after starting because the ultimate goal is too far in the future.

Instead, I'm going to help you set the bar in a different way. We're going to isolate the most important goals and wishes that you have and that you've been putting on hold. We're going to tie that into the four areas you assessed your life choices in up to this point (your health, your relationships, your contribution, and your personal growth). Doing so will allow you to create goals that you can absolutely achieve in 90 days, so you will experience growth, renewal, and, most importantly, momentum.

In Section 3, we'll create mind maps for each of these areas, so you have the freedom to think and imagine everything that you possibly want to do. Then I will show you how to prioritize those goals, so you have structure to them. Rather than a seemingly endless bucket list, you will know what goals are most important to you and what areas of your life those goals will enhance.

The second way we'll focus on how to avoid regrets in life revolves around how you view yourself, and building a strong, positive mindset.

In Section 2, we will dive deep into the biggest thing that holds everyone back, and that is fear. I will challenge you to answer questions like "how do I perceive myself" and "how can I look at myself in a positive, loving way?" I will help you isolate the fears and negative self-talk that is holding you back from being the authentic person you really are.

If you change anything as the result of our journey together, let it be the way you view yourself, because if you can look back at the end of your life loving who you are, then your life will be a success, no matter what you do. The work we will do in the chapters ahead will be designed to rebuild your mindset from an optimistic, motivated place, so you act with courage and conviction, rather than be stuck by fear rooted in self-doubt.

In this chapter, we're going to look at how to predict regrets based on what you are doing with your time, *as well as how you're NOT spending your time.*

Predicting regrets starts by determining what you are saying "no" to for yourself. What are you putting on hold in your life right now?

On the surface, this question is everything. It's the summation of what regrets are about and how to avoid them. It's the opportunity to look at what you really want as opposed to what you don't.

People don't give themselves enough permission to think about what they want. As we become adults, we get buried by obligations, responsibilities, tasks, deadlines, overbooked schedules, and distractions, so the last thing we create time for is evaluating ourselves. To further complicate things, you may have influences throughout your life that have taught you that thinking about what you want is bad, negative, selfish, even ego-centric, so you have become trained to put others' needs in front of our own. *(More on this in Section 2: Getting Selfish.)*

Looking at what you want in life can feel like an overwhelming starting point. It's easier to actually start first with what you *don't want*, as opposed to what you do, and then build awareness from there.

Let's use an example to illustrate this...

Think of the last time you were with a group of friends trying to decide what type of food to grab for dinner. What typically happens in this situation? Someone will throw out the question, "hey what are you in the mood for?" The more people in the group, the more stammering and silence as everyone thinks through all the different restaurants in the area, asking themselves, "what do I really want?" This exercise can become time-consuming and a bit exhausting because no one is speaking their mind on what they really want.

But imagine how this would play out if, instead of asking "what are you in the mood for," you ask, "what *don't you want* for dinner?" If you haven't tried it, do it as an experiment. Watch and observe what happens. Your friends will start to say all the things they don't want, and instantly the decision on where to go for dinner becomes easier because you can start to use the process of elimination until the group comes to a consensus.

Since the future can feel uncertain when getting ready to embark on change, the different choices and paths in front of you can feel overwhelming. If you haven't said "yes" to yourself in a long time, then it can seem even more challenging. So it's easier to first look at what you don't want. What's not working for you. What have you experienced in the past that you don't want to repeat. This will be your starting point.

When applying this to your own life, start by asking yourself this:

1. What don't I want in my life?

2. What will I no longer accept as a part of my life?

Reflect on the map of choices you created in Chapter 2 and the consequences as a result that you discovered in Chapter 3. What is it that you don't want that those choices brought into your life? These questions are fundamental, because understanding what you don't want will help you find the clarity to determine what you *really want*, because it's the complete opposite.

Living a life of "don't wants" and "shoulds" is what leads to regrets later down the road. Being able to understand what those things are both in your current life and in past chapters of your life will help you predict your regrets later on and actually avoid them from ever happening.

It's the things that you *really want* that are the things you will want to take action on, so you can avoid regrets all together. You will not regret the things that you did do, but you will regret the things that you didn't do that you wish you had.

- If you want the freedom of being your own boss, then you will want to act on creating a plan to leave your job, so you can start your own business.

- If you want a healthy, lean, and strong body, then you will want to eliminate bad habits and start to challenge yourself physically.

- If you want to have more travel and adventure in your life, then you will want to think about ways to have more of that now and create a plan for the experiences you want to have.

Use your past as a GPS in this process, too. We can all look to things we have done in our past that we wish we wouldn't have done or wish we could have done differently. What are those for you? Why do you feel that way about those periods or decisions in your life? Knowing this will help you avoid repeating them and also to understand more of what's important to you.

If I could take the current version of me now and go back to that 26-year-old version of me, who just became a doctor and spent the next six months looking for the high-paying job in a booming practice, I would tell her, "It's not all about the job.

> *Just go out to the mountains like you want, even if you don't have the job yet. You fell in love with New*

Zealand and its natural beauty. You can recreate that way of life in the States. It's what made you happy. Don't worry about the achievements or the security or the success for now. Trust yourself and you will figure it out. You always do. Focus on the bigger picture. Learn how to become a bartender or something else in the meantime to make money, and it'll all sort itself out in the end. You love being spontaneous, so take a risk. It's what your free-spirited part of you would want to do. You'll find it out there. You know you'll be happy out there. Don't get so attached to the grades or the loans. Listen to what your heart is telling you and go travel and explore."

That would've changed the course of everything. I wouldn't have spent seven years living in a big, stressful city. I wouldn't have spent seven years dealing with burnout, depression, and a yearning to just get out in nature. But I couldn't because, well, I was attached to my job, my practice, my patients, and the people who were in my life there.

I don't look back at that time with regret, because in those struggles, I experienced so much growth and awareness of what I wanted.

I also know that there are powerful lessons that I gathered during that time. It makes me appreciate what I have now, because I have so much more clarity in who I am and what I want out of life. I now have more outdoor adventure, travel, and freedom in my life because of it, and I didn't want to wake up in the end wishing I had woken up and done something different.

If you've found yourself saying, "I wish I could do this" or "I have to wait until I retire to do this," recognize that those are the future regrets that you will have if you don't act on them now. Not tomorrow. Not next week. Not next year. Now.

As you can see, the way of life from my past was very different from the way I live now. I used my experiences to determine what I didn't want, so I could create a way of life that fostered more fulfillment on a continual basis, rather than settling for the way of life I had.

Never settle for the present if it's holding you back from a happier future.

As you look at the things in your life that you don't want, now start to reflect on what is the opposite. Looking at your life from both sides of the spectrum like this will help you compare what you don't want in your life now to what you do want in the future. The gap in-between is what we will fill during your 90-Day Life Challenge.

Now let's look to the opposite and what you want instead.

What are those things for you? The things that if today was your last day, you would look back on with regret, wishing that you would have done? Is there a goal you've had that you keep putting off? Let your brain get creative in this process. Think about the crazy, wild, and big ideas that you've had that are now stashed away in the archives of your mind. When you see these dreams staring you in the face again, it's hard to ignore them. When you become aware on a different level, you know more of what you want, you act differently, and you do better.

That is the power you will discover in your 90-Day Life Challenge. You act with a heightened sense of awareness and purpose, because you know what you've been putting on hold and stop the waiting game, purposefully.

So, you don't have to look back and wish "if only I had done this sooner." Instead, you can look back at the end with satisfaction and a smile, knowing that you really went for it.

What a gift it is to be able to do that no matter what stage of life you're in right now. You are choosing to live on a higher level, purely because you are giving yourself the freedom to focus on it.

The "Ping"

In moments where we look at our lives and realize that something is missing, we often look outside of ourselves to what others have, because it is easier to look outward than within.

Think of a moment in your life when you saw someone who had something that you wish you had. Maybe that person had a better job, better house, better marriage, better health, or a better body.

What did you feel in that moment witnessing that person? Did you feel envious or jealous because they have something that you coveted? If you did, that's because you are saying "no" to something that you want within yourself, and it's easier to project that frustration onto them than it is to accept that within yourself.

It's within our nature to compare ourselves with others in some way. Some would say that comes from instinct and our desire to be at the top in the "survival of the fittest." Others may say that this has become more prevalent over time in a society that is more based on "instant gratification," which is teaching us to want more, to want to be important, and to want what others have.

In my opinion, it's because it is easier to compare ourselves to others than compare ourselves to what we wish for ourselves. It's easy to look to others and wish we had what they have, rather than look at why we feel that way and why this is important to us.

When you look to what others have that you desire, what it really reflects is something that you feel is missing within your own life. This is a phenomenon that I like to call the "ping."

It's that moment when your heart aches and stops for a moment because you see someone experiencing or possessing something in life that you don't currently have. It could be people who have a bigger paycheck, house, or investment portfolio — or a smaller waistline.

When I decided to sell my possessions and live out of my suitcase, I noticed something interesting in my interactions with people. While striking up a conversation with someone, oftentimes one of the first questions asked was, "where are you from?" or "where do you live?" With my lifestyle, that answer was a bit unique. After enough times of trying to figure out how to answer it, I started to reply with this: "I live nowhere, and I live anywhere, anytime I choose."

Naturally, that created more questions from people, asking me things like, "how do you do that? How can I do that?"

But the most common reaction I would get is: "Oh you're so lucky. I wish I could do that!"

In that comment I realized something: the person across from me felt like life was happening to them, so they couldn't change it. They created a trap and couldn't look past it to see that they could create the very same way of life. This reaction reflects more about the person's beliefs of what they're capable of than what they can ACTUALLY do in their lives.

I used to respond to replies like this with a moment of gratitude and something to the extent of, "Thank you. I feel really lucky to be able to do this." But then I just realized that all this was doing was reinforcing the very beliefs that these people were showing me, which was in essence:

This sounds great, but I could never do it.

Once I realized this, my answers started to change, because I realized something very important. I was their "ping." I was living a life they coveted but never thought possible, and I have never been in a place like this before.

Here's why I'm sharing this story with you:

This didn't just "happen" to me overnight. I didn't just sell my practice and my possessions and grow a thriving online business overnight. Nothing in my life ever materialized overnight. It was a series of decisions, actions, wake-up calls, and course corrections that made it happen, and all of that took time, a ton of awareness, and a hunger for change.

Five years prior, I could barely pay the rent, was living in a not-so-great neighborhood in D.C., with $150,000 of student loans weighing me down. I couldn't take off time to visit family, let alone call in sick without getting docked. I had no power in my life. My life was the consequence of a lot of bad decisions that I wouldn't make today.

When it comes to avoiding regrets, you have to decide on one of two things: Settle and struggle, or break away and create change.

We are not the side effect of our current circumstances. We are the CAUSE of them. Once you realize that you had the power to create the way of life you're in right now, you'll see that you have the same power to change it.

What the "pings" should do is create a desire within us to change, rather than just wish, want, or hope for something that we don't feel like we'll ever get. Feeling that way won't get you anywhere.

When I recognized the power of the "ping," I realized that there were other pings I was ignoring.

Like the "ping I would feel when I would see a successful entrepreneur on the speaking circuit and wish I was the one on the stage. Or the "ping" I would feel when hearing stories of long-lost friends from college doing hiking adventures and exploring the world.

The "ping" can create a lifetime of yearning or a life of action. It's ultimately up to us what we decide to do with it.

The gaps that you see in your life are a combination of action, lack of action, or misguided action. You will never create the life you want to have if you spend the majority of your time yearning, searching, waiting, or wishing for something.

Pings can be a source for regret, or fuel for more action.

It's your opportunity to transform your "pings" from a source of future regret into fuel to power a state of consistent, focused action to step into the life you've been wanting to live.

The ping is a part of your answer to what's missing in your life. It's an opportunity for you to recognize where you are happy in your life, and where you are dissatisfied. The people who come into your life, who have something you want, should be seen as a source of inspiration and fuel to create the same for yourself.

That is the power of the ping.

Now It's Your Turn:

1. What are the "pings" in your life? Think about things you wish to have, be, or do that you currently lack.

2. *Oftentimes, there will be people that you think of who do have these things in their life. Think about them and how they can be a source of inspiration for you.*

3. Understanding this will help you determine, what are the dreams that you have said no to in your life so far? *This is an opportunity now to recognize what's missing.*

4. Now ask, how would my future look if I listened to the pings from within and took action on them?

The Child Within You

Remember that feeling as a kid, where your imagination went wild? You could do anything and be anything.

I remember playing basketball on my parents' farm thinking of making the game-winning shot. I remember gazing up at the skies and seeing the stars overhead, dreaming of what it would be like to be amongst them.

I didn't question anything. I didn't instantly let fears slip in and tell me it wasn't possible. Because in my mind, everything was possible.

What did that feel like for you?

Think about when you were a child when the opportunities felt endless. The whole world felt like it was right in front of you. Your life was just beginning.

The childlike wonder of wishing and dreaming is a beautiful, blissful place that we all find ourselves at times wishing to go back to, but think that time is lost as we grew into the responsibilities of adulthood.

But it's only because we've let our own self-taught or self-imposed obligations, insecurities, and fears get in our way. We let our minds become our opponent, rather than our ally and a force rooting us on.

This plants the seeds of regrets because we let go of the reckless abandon we had as children.

In looking to your future, you can bring that sense of wonder and possibility back into your mind in an instant. Just like when you catch yourself daydreaming during a quiet time during a picnic, or looking up in the clouds.

You can let your mind go there. It's not a place long gone. It's just a place that you've allowed yourself to forget, a destination you've lost the directions for.

So, you need to tap back into that world without barriers, limiting beliefs, or uncertainties getting in your way, and just dream again. You need to go back to pure possibilities, because your true self and a wildly happy life lies in that space.

It's time to talk to your inner child again, that part of your mind that can wish for anything, imagine anything, dream of anything, hope for anything, and believe in anything to create a big, beautiful future for yourself.

Now you might be thinking, "but I have all these responsibilities, I don't have time to think like this, it's useless. I'm too old for that. I don't know if I can. I'm scared to try."

That's where you get stuck.

It's not that you have to cast away your responsibilities or get reckless. It's that you have to allow your brain to wander, hope, and wish again.

You have to give yourself permission to see that you can have both. You will naturally have responsibilities, obligations, things to tend to, take care of, and love.

But that doesn't mean you have to let the responsibilities of life drag you down to feeling helpless, hopeless, or stuck. You have the right to look at those responsibilities from a place of joy, while retaining the ability to create whatever way you choose to take care of the responsibilities that matter to you the most.

We all need money, a roof over our heads, people who love us, people we love, and a sense of purpose. But we don't need to face these things with drudgery or fatigue because "that's just the way life is."

You can have all those things while pursuing new opportunities, growth, and happiness.

Talk to your inner child for a moment right now, and ask yourself this, "If you could do anything, literally anything in your life, what would you want to do?"

What's the first thing that comes to your mind?

Allow yourself to feel that sense of awe and wonder again. The point here is to think without limits and think of what ideas come to your mind that create a spark of excitement.

Take out your workbook now or a blank piece of paper, write down the first thing that comes to mind for you, and then answer the following questions?

- How long have you wanted to do this?
- Why does this excite you?
- How would your life feel if you made it happen?

Be creative. Be open. Find a quiet space and let your mind wander. If you hear that voice in your head telling you that this is ridiculous or impossible, that's a good sign that this is something you need to listen to, because your adult brain has clouded your ability to imagine and dream.

Your mind knows what's missing. Your mind knows what you've been putting on hold. You've just allowed yourself to choose to not think of that because at some point in your life you told yourself it wasn't possible and you moved on.

In these questions, you will find your clarity in what you've been putting on the back burner.

Without tapping into our inner child, we wake up in life letting time and our dreams slip by, without giving ourselves a chance of being able to even get a taste of what experiencing that dream could feel like.

Now, if you're feeling stuck here, take a moment to actually picture yourself during a younger time in your life. Go back to that time when you were just playing, having fun, and being free. Go to that version of you. What are you doing? How did you play? What were you curious and excited about? *What activities do you recall from your childhood or being a adolescent or teen even now that you could do and lose track of time because you love it so much?*

Take a moment to rediscover what these things are. You may find it helpful to actually reach out to old friends and relatives to revisit memories from earlier in life, so they can remind you of what you were like, what you loved, what you were obsessed with during that time. This is where our lost "roots" are to be found. Back then, if we had an itch, we found a way to scratch it.

If you are like most people, you will find yourself flooded with memories of the toys you loved to play with, what made you laugh, what you wanted to be when you grew up, and how you loved spending your days. The moment you become aware of these things again and take yourself back to that way of being that is free, playful, and imaginative is the moment you can start to bring that back into your life.

Think about the qualities of what you loved to do when you were younger and how you can bring more of this into your life today.

*"You will find more happiness
growing down than up."*

— UNKNOWN

You are never too old, too broke, or too uncertain to tap back into what you want out of life. You can wish, dream, and hope right now, if you choose.

Your inner child is where your imagination and ability to dream can come alive. You start to see again what is possible for you and what you are capable of.

While tapping into your inner child won't change your life instantly, what it will do is change your view on life instantly and propel you to take action on the dreams you have buried.

Will you become a fitness model overnight? Will you travel the world overnight? Or build a million-dollar business overnight? No, but you can take steps in that direction, any direction, in an instant.

By purely taking action, we put ourselves one step closer to making our dreams happen. Now here is where action really happens...

If you only had 90 days to take action toward your dreams, what would you do with that time? This is what we'll uncover in Section 3. Looking at your dreams with a specific timeframe gives you the opportunity to choose what you want to do with the time that is given.

Waking up realizing that you aren't fully living into your dreams is a powerful awakening, and it can be one of the most important times of your life, because you will no longer just tell yourself:

"I'll get to that later."

"I don't have the time for this right now."

"I'll never get to this. My time has already passed."

Because it's giving you the opportunity to create a choice.

Do you fall victim to your current situation, responsibilities, state of happiness, and life? Or do you take ownership of what brought you here, to this place right now, and commit to shifting it?

So, you can remember those deep dreams within you and create the momentum to make them happen.

Turning Regrets into Action

To go from living the life you're telling yourself you HAVE to live to pursuing the life that you WANT, complete this exercise before going into Section 2.

1. What do you wish you could do? Be? Have? Achieve? Create? What are the dreams that you have been putting on hold? *Let your mind wander without fear or limitation. Focus only on the endless possibilities you can create in your life, with the same awe and wonder you had as a child.*

2. Why are these dreams important to you? Why have you been putting them off?

3. What would that version of yourself look like if you made this happen?

4. If you only had 90 days to take action toward your dreams, what would you do with that time?

SECTION 2:

A NEW STATE OF MIND FOR A NEW WAY OF LIFE

Break away from the patterns that have held you back and create the life you really want.

CHAPTER 5:

BREAKING AWAY FROM YOUR COMFORT ZONE

"A comfort zone is a beautiful place,
but nothing ever grows there."

— UNKNOWN

THERE IS A gap between who you are now and who you want to become. Who you are now is your comfort zone. It's called the comfort zone for a reason.

Your comfort zone is a culmination of everything that is a constant in your life, from your routines, to your habits, to your thoughts, to your behaviors. Comfort allows you to do the things that need to get done without conscious thought. It also allows you to run your life on autopilot when necessary. It's what you know. It's what you've known for some time, and it's easy to stay there.

Comfort can be a good thing. Comfort can come in the form of a home, material possessions, a warm blanket, a cup of coffee, our loved ones, stability of a job and a paycheck, and our day-to-day life. With comfort comes predictability. We know who we are, what we do, when we do it, and what to expect. Comfort allows us to get more things done during the day. It allows us to anticipate what is coming next based on past experiences and outcomes. We know what we're going to think and how we're going to act in a given situation all because of the comfort we have built to surround us.

With comfort comes stability. When the stability nourishes you and keeps you happy, then it serves you. When it allows you to be your most productive self, then it supports you.

Comfort is also part of the reason why people feel more unfulfilled in their lives than ever before. That's when comfort is being used as a crutch and isn't really serving you. Comfort can keep you stuck in old ideas, negative habits, self-limiting thoughts, and self-defeating behaviors, because this is also what you know. When comfort manifests in these ways, it will keep you safe from acting differently from what you know and keep you stuck.

Section 2 is all about breaking away from comfort that isn't serving you. It's about recognizing where the constants of comfort can be a bad thing and seeing how comfort, when misplaced, can hold you back from the happiness and life you crave. Once you understand this, you can open your mind to opportunity and change.

To recap Section 1 briefly, I introduced the art of impermanence to you and how to choose that as a way of life, so you can make the most of the time that is in front of you right now. We looked at your choices and the consequences of those choices, as well as how those things have created your life today, so you can determine what it is that is serving you well and what is not. We looked at the power of regrets and how to predict them, so you can act in accordance with what you really want in life, rather than the way of life you've been told and believe you're supposed to live.

We created an opportunity for you to look deeply into your life to reflect on what's bringing you joy, what's holding you back, and what you have been putting off. We did this to help bring your dreams and what's important to you to the forefront, so you can start to make them a priority in your life and take action on them in your 90-Day Life Challenge.

In this section and stage of our journey, I will introduce a second core principle and that's the principle of novelty. To break away from comfort, you must learn to embrace change. People tend to fear change because change is uncertain. It can be terrifying because it can take you away from what you know. It's why people will spend years in a job, relationship, level of health, financial position, and state of mind that's not making them happy because they are comforted by it, even if they don't enjoy it.

I've worked with so many people over the years who are tired of where they are in life, but terrified to snap out of it. They have grown so accustomed to the place they are in that they have let it become their identity and their fate. They don't see the long-term impact that staying comfortable can have in their life because they are blinded by the stability it provides.

Section 1 was intended as a wake-up call for you. Section 2 is designed to light a fire under you.

We are going to prime you for your 90-Day Life Challenge by:

- Building a new mindset so you can think big and dream big.
- Learning the fears that hold you back, so you can crush them.
- Bridging the gap from your present life to the life you want.
- Discovering how to put yourself and your priorities first again to create an enriching life.
- Silencing self-limiting thoughts and creating a new set linked to behaviors that will serve you to grow.

Get Comfortable with Getting Uncomfortable

Before I ask you to look internally to find where comfort isn't serving you, I want to address how things outside of you can keep you comfortable in a way that isn't serving you.

Any new change, challenge, or journey is bound to bring a sense of discomfort. I'm going to help you expect it and teach you how to channel it, so you don't fall under the power of it and let it stop you in your tracks. Whether it's doubts in your own mind or hearing criticism from others, you will face moments when you question what you are doing.

I believe resistance comes into our lives for a reason. It shows up at a time when we actually need it the most. It's a test for us to cement what we really want to commit to.

Inherently, when we are going after something we want, there is bound to be some type of struggle. That is where you find your strength. Your determination. Your resilience.

Tearing down the walls of comfort takes courage. You will face fears that have trapped you, beliefs that have held you back, and habits that have limited you. When you seek to make changes in your life and create a path less traveled, you will encounter resistance, both from within yourself, as well as from others around you.

That's why I want to give you the heads-up as you maneuver into making changes in your life, *because the naysayers will come knocking.*

There will be people in your life who will try to hold you back from change, for they too, are comfortable. They know you as you are. They are used to it, accustomed to it, and they will resist that change in return. They may question you. They may challenge you. They may not support you in the way you expect. They may think your dreams are too farfetched, too outlandish, or too impossible to achieve. Or simply, not good for *them.*

What you need to understand if this happens is that this is not about their opinion of you. This is about what they actually believe to be true about themselves and how they see the world. When someone sees something as impossible, that is their reality, not your own.

If you encounter this, it's not personal. Someone's criticism isn't a reflection of you, who you are, or what you really want in life or *can do* in life.

It's a reflection of that person and how they see the world — and themselves. It's their perception being projected onto you. Nothing more. Nothing less. It doesn't mean they don't love you or care about you. But it also doesn't mean that they know what's best for you better than you do, or that they have the power to hold you back.

We all have a different lens through which we see the world and ourselves.

Don't let the opinions of others choose the path in front of you. You have to get comfortable with getting uncomfortable.

Ben's family adores him. In fact, anyone who is blessed to cross his path adores him. He is a kind, loving, outgoing man, the type of person who wears his heart on his sleeve. You get that instant feeling that he would do anything for the people he loves in an instant.

Ben is also an inspiration. At the age of 74, he has hiked more mountains and more miles than anyone I know who is half his age. I had the good fortune of meeting him on his way down from the summit of Mount Timpanogos, which sits at an elevation of 11,752 feet (3582 meters). This summit was a goal of mine, as I had attempted this trail twice the year prior, and the mountain won. I was bound and determined to make the third hike the charm.

As I approach the saddle section of the trail, I'm already close to an elevation of about 10,000 ft. The air is thinner. Each step feels heavier, and I feel my breath quicken as I trudge along. Below me is a green valley filled with meadows and fading blooms hinting that summer is coming to a close, while the area in front of me now is rugged, rocky, and arid. The trail beneath my feet that started soft and cushioned by a thin blanket of pine needles has turned to jagged, slate rock. The summit hut is but a point on the horizon, but it's what drives me to keep going.

I see a man clad in khaki pants and a white cotton shirt effortlessly bounding down the trail with a grin that spanned ear-to-ear. I had never seen anyone so happy after enduring a summit, and I had a gut feeling that this must be the "awesome old guy" who everyone talks about on this trail.

Ben was descending from his 922nd summit of Mt Timp. No, that's not a typo. At the time I crossed paths with him, he had been up and down that mountain nine hundred and twenty-two times. What's even more astonishing is that once he completed it, he was going to do summit #923 that very same day. This type of hike is known as "the double."

At the time of writing this sentence, he had just finished #955. That's 14,325 miles (23,053 kilometers) of hiking in a span of just a few years. For perspective, that's the same distance as walking around our moon 2.5 times.

As Ben approached his retirement age a few years back, he questioned what he would do in the next chapter of his life. "I've seen so many people in my life get less active the older they get. Almost everyone in my family is unfit and spends their free time watching TV. I knew I didn't want to be like that, so I just started hiking," he told me.

Our brief chat during his descent spoke volumes of his desire to stay out of the comfort zone, even though he was surrounded by opportunities to do so. Ben's family challenged him. They questioned his love for hiking. They thought he was crazy and would say things to him like, "When are you going to stop hiking? Aren't you getting too old for this???"

Ben could have settled for his family's opinions of what was best for him. He could've gotten comfortable. He could've sat idle because it was an easy, safe decision, and one that he saw the people he loved the most making on a daily basis. He could have chosen the safety of doing what everyone else was doing, and he could have found great comfort in that.

He also would have slowly let his will, his desire, and his passion for life erode.

Imagine how sad that would have been. Think about the regrets Ben could have faced in his final stages of life if he chose comfort over risk, the couch over the trail, security over courage, and safety over fearlessness.

But Ben didn't do that. He didn't want comfortable. He didn't want easy, and he didn't want safe. His spirit wanted adventure. He body wanted to be pushed. He had limits he wanted to break. He wanted to continue to feel young and challenge the belief that at some point you are too old to thrive and "you have to just watch life go by."

"I didn't want to just go home and sit. There is so much more to do in life." After he shared this, I shook Ben's hand and watched this agile man run effortlessly into the valley below. Within seconds his body was out of sight, but the impact he made on me would stay forever.

Ben chose uncomfortable. He chose to not let the naysayers drag him down, even though those naysayers were people very near and dear to him.

He put himself first. He listened to the crazy goals in his head, and he went for it. Now his goal is to hike Mount Timp every year as many times as his age. He has already done it four years in a row, and every time he reaches a new hundredth milestone, the local media comes out to celebrate him. People on the trail give him hugs, high fives, and praise *all because he chose uncomfortable*. He didn't let his age define him. Instead, he took the path less traveled by continually pushing himself.

Ben and I in August 2017

When the naysayers show up as you make a new commitment in your life, look at this as an opportunity to build certainty on your "why." Why you are doing what you are doing. Why you are committing to the changes you are making. Why you are setting out on this new path.

These people show up in your life for a reason. To challenge you. To question you. To help you build your own sense of self-growth and ownership. Be grateful in your mind for these people. It can be natural at first to feel defensive, or worse, dis-empowered and follow the pack and what others think is best for you.

Instead, you can seize this as an opportunity to hold your ground and reaffirm what matters to you, regardless of what anyone else thinks.

What Uncomfortable Means to You

Along this journey, there will be thoughts, ideas, and people that inspire you, and others that will hold you back and try to keep you comfortable, safe, and stuck. We'll address how to overcome the fears and beliefs stowed in your mind in upcoming chapters, but for now, I want you to linger on this idea of getting uncomfortable.

You have the opportunity to stop being comfortable in ways that don't serve you, so you can create a version of yourself that can be ecstatic to get out of bed in the morning. A version that doesn't say no to the things you want to create in life and take action. A version that starts to really own what you are capable of.

Breaking out of your comfort zone is what will create the space and energy for you to focus on the new. Bringing new stimuli into your life, creating new ideas, and taking new actions. You'll notice that once you're no longer comfortable, you are more open to the opportunities in front of you. In fact, you will also start to recognize comforts that support you and ones that hinder you, and you'll create a sense of restlessness that will translate into action, rather than a lack thereof.

Now let me ask you a few questions about what uncomfortable means to you:

1. What are the thoughts, actions, and habits in your day-to-day life that feel comfortable, but actually hold you back? Consider what you routinely say to yourself and do on a regular basis.

2. Think of a time in your life when you didn't listen to a naysayer and stood your ground for what you wanted. How did that feel? What positive effect did you experience as a result?

Novelty is Our Nature

"The joy of life comes from our encounters
with new experiences, and hence
there is no greater joy than to have an
endlessly changing horizon, for each
day to have a new and different sun."

— JON KRAKAUER, INTO THE WILD

There is a war happening in your brain right now. On one side of the battlefield is monotony. This is your opponent, and it's the part of your mind that likes consistency. Your mind is wired in feedback loops. It's designed to run automatically, so you don't have to think about what you are doing most of the time. Your conscious mind likes this. It's easy to function in life this way. It's good to use for the things that we shouldn't have to think about, like brushing our teeth or doing the dishes, but it will cleverly mask itself in routine in all arenas. It will cloud your ambitions. It will tell you sameness is a good thing. It's not exciting, but it's stable. It's predictable. It comforts you.

But life wasn't meant to be monotonous. A boring life is a wasted life. It's death of the human spirit. Life was meant to be stimulating to the senses, filled with wonder and awe.

The good news for you is that monotony has one weakness. This weakness is its kryptonite, and if you can tap into and summon the powers of this, it will defeat monotony forever. That weakness is known as novelty.

nov·el·ty

the quality of being new, original, or unusual.

Think about a time in your life where you experienced something new — seeing a new place, tasting a new type of food, meeting someone you felt instant chemistry with. When your brain gets exposed to a new stimulus or environment, it goes into sensory overload. All the feedback loops of monotony stop firing, and instead, parts of your brain wake up and come alive. Your energy heightens. You become more alert, and you are in a state of bliss.

Novelty is at the root of what we as humans crave, and research[6] has actually now shown why this is the case.

C. Robert Cloninger, a psychiatrist and avid researcher of novelty, has found that "novelty-seeking is one of the traits that keeps you healthy, happy, and fosters personality growth as you age."

Novelty encourages you to keep life fresh and interesting, so you don't get stuck in the comforts of routine.

Everyone wants to grow old, but no one wants to feel old, and novelty is the fountain of youth. Youth is curious because so much is unknown. Youth is adventure-seeking because there is no fear. Youth is playful because life isn't taken seriously.

People who live a life of monotony are unconsciously seeking novelty all the time, they just don't see it. It's why people "rubberneck" during an accident on the highway. Their interest is piqued, so they stop and look, never minding the traffic jam they are causing. Commuting is boring. People coast from point A to point B automatically, sometimes without even being able to recount how they got there. But when a fender-bender occurs taking two cars to the side of the road, everyone slows enough to gape as they go by. Why? It's novel, yes; our curiosity is piqued.

People are seeking novelty all the time. It's why we love the quick high when a two-day delivery arrives at our door. It's why we love following the latest trend or fad, and get excited by the headlines from the evening news.

This isn't novelty in the truest sense, though. It's the Band-Aid version of novelty. Something a little sticky that people can tack onto themselves to feel less monotonous, even for a moment, but it's external. They aren't creating it. They are seeking it in others, and then applying it to themselves to make it feel like it's their own.

Novelty at its core gives YOU the opportunity to cultivate new experiences, break through some of your own personal barriers and fears, and come out on the other side of it a little wiser and braver.

Novelty is the very thing that keeps us from being too safe. Because safe means the same and the same means stuck. If you're not evolving through life, you're stuck in life.

Journalist Winifred Gallagher shared in her recent research, "Now: Understanding Our Need for Novelty and Change,"[7] how novelty is actually essential for human survival. The desire for novelty is what allows us as humans to seek out adventures, undiscovered resources, and untapped opportunities that wouldn't exist without this psychological desire.

Interestingly enough, Winifred's findings showed that the more novelty we have in our lives, the happier we are with our lives. Moments of novelty actually change the chemistry of the brain and release the neurotransmitter dopamine, which creates feelings of happiness, satisfaction, and joy.

People with more novelty and spontaneity in their lives are shown to flourish in their health, relationships, and overall life satisfaction. Why? Because deep within each of us, we crave the new, whether that's new ideas, things, or experiences.

The challenge within our society today is that novelty has been masked in *things* above everything else. It's why there is chaos during Black Friday sales and lines around the block to get the latest smartphone. It's why the phrase "shopping therapy" exists. Sales, promotions, and things give us the same dose of joy and sense of euphoria that novelty has been shown to produce.

There is nothing inherently wrong with short bursts of happiness that material things can bring into our lives, but what these things will not do, that novelty can do, is deliver *sustainable joy over time*.

The problem is that the high is very short-lived when material things or other things outside of yourself are your source of novelty. We've become a culture of instant gratification, looking for the next quick dose of euphoria, and we're bombarded with it everywhere. From tweets and posts to what's trending to being hooked to our devices, our days have become filled with bursts of doing stuff or getting stuff.

What we're missing is the ability to create long-term satisfaction throughout our lives and in every day. We need to reclaim the ability to actually find the happiness within ourselves and control how we choose to spend our time, rather than seeking things to fill that gap.

True novelty is a rare commodity now because our lives are more filled with busywork, projects, obligations, deadlines, and distractions, yet it's something we can create so easily in our lives, if we just choose to.

You will see in later chapters how part of enriching your life in just 90 days comes down to the *experiences you create*, for they will be more valuable than any one thing you can purchase or acquire. Experiences, momentum, and personal growth are all different sources of novelty that will create a cumulative effect of a new, happier version of you that will last for the long-term.

The lives we create are also all a result of a culmination of little decisions. Our self-worth, finances, weight, relationships, environment, everything is based on either staying stuck or creating novelty.

If you find yourself dissatisfied with the amount of money you make, the amount of love you have, the amount of health in your life, it's partly because novelty is missing.

Because novelty sparks change, and when you combine the joy of novelty with the urgency of impermanence, you will quickly see that the one choice in front of you is to act differently than you are right now, which will propel you to break away from the routines of your day-to-day life and the ways of thinking that are holding you back, so you can redefine you who really are and want to become.

Routines should serve us to be consistent in purposeful actions and behaviors, so you don't have to constantly think of everything you need to do in a day. But novelty — call it curiosity if you prefer —will bring the spice of life to keep those routines fresh while adding spontaneity to your life. You want to use routines mindfully, so you don't get caught on "life autopilot."

And in case you're wondering, novelty doesn't have to come from doing something epic. It's not like you have to go skydiving one day and bungee jumping the next. You can find novelty in the simple things, like bringing fresh flowers to your home or shopping at a new store in your neighborhood.

You'll get the same sense of euphoria either way. Your brain will create the same reaction no matter how small or grand the novel action.

Recognize that the more novelty that you create in your life, the more you will inherently seek, desire, and create growth and joy.

Building Your Novelty Muscles

In your 90-Day Life Challenge, you are going to elevate the level at which you think and act on a consistent basis. The journey in and of itself will be brimming with novelty.

In the upcoming three chapters, we are going to look within you and deconstruct the thoughts, beliefs, and habits that have been holding you back and keeping you too comfortable.

But for now, I want to get you accustomed to the process of transitioning from monotony to bringing more novelty into your life, so let's start with a simple exercise:

- First, I want you map out your daily routine. Think about all the things that you do consistently on a day-to-day basis. This should be very detailed, down to the simple tasks from when you take a shower to when you eat lunch. Think about what time of the day you do these things and how you do them. I call this practice *routine flushing* because you're basically going to deconstruct your routine and then flush the monotony down the drain, so your day-to-day life can start to have a spark to it again.

Think of this process like writing out a recipe, where you list what you do every day (aka "the ingredients") and then you write out in order when you do these tasks (like the steps for cooking the meal).

Once you have your routine mapped out, you can actually see where all the potential sources of monotony lie in your everyday life.

- Now, I want you to pick one of the items in your list. Look at that item and ask yourself, "How can I do this one thing differently today compared to yesterday?"

Here are some ideas to help you brainstorm:

  - Try a new recipe for dinner.
  - Watch a different channel.
  - Go outside to have lunch rather than sit at your desk.
  - Take a different route home from work.
  - Do a new exercise at the gym.
  - Sleep on the opposite side of the bed.
  - Listen to a new song.

Just start with changing one item in your routine for now, so you can see how simple it is to switch from monotony to novelty.

This simple practice in novelty can create a sense of spontaneity and spark in your life – so you can experience something new and get an instant dose of joy purely from doing something that is automatic a little bit differently.

You will soon discover that there may be a number of things that you do in your day-to-day routine because you have gotten used to them, or they've just become a habit. While routines can help bring consistency and help make the most of our time, we do not want to lose the joys that come from throwing in some novel concepts or ideas that can keep your life fresh and exciting.

Experiment with this simple exercise and see how one small step can create a spark of joy that will change the course of your day and ultimately the course of your life.

CHAPTER 6:

DEFEATING SELF-SABOTAGE

"Only as high as I reach can I grow, only as far as I seek can I go, only as deep as I look can I see, only as much as I dream can I be."

— KAREN RAVN

I'M A SUCKER for a good burger, and the first bite is always the best. I hardly eat any fast food these days, but when I do, that's my guilty pleasure. What can I say, I'm a farm girl from Wisconsin. Burgers and brats are like a major food group where I'm from.

Of course, when I get a burger, I can't just get a single patty. Oh no. I have to get all of the fixins. Double patty with cheese and bacon, lettuce, tomato, mayo, pickles and everything else in-between. I like my burger sitting so tall that I have to press it down to take a bite.

Then I take my first bite, and it's glorious. The burger is juicy. The bacon is crispy. The bun holds everything together just perfectly. It's like a carnival ride of tastes in my mouth, and I'm in bliss. I instantly feel satisfied.

My taste buds want more. I'm ready for the next salty, greasy bite now that the first one is under my belt, and it tastes amazing. Oddly though, it doesn't taste quite as amazing as the first bite did. Still satisfying, but the flavors don't stand out as much, but I keep chowing down, lingering on the euphoria that first bite gave me.

By the time I'm left with just a few bites, reality sinks in. I feel the weight of the grease in my gut. My breath starts to smell like onions. I think I have a ring of ketchup around my mouth and grab more napkins. I start to get a little sleepy, and my stomach starts to churn. What's even worse is that I start to beat myself up. Rather than enjoy the burger for what it is, I go down a litany of thoughts to make me feel bad about this little guilty pleasure. "Why do I keep doing this to myself? Don't I have any self-control? I really didn't *need* this burger. I feel so fat. I'm never going to lose this weight."

I know these thoughts will come, because I have been down this road before, several times over. It's a two-week cycle that goes something like this: Wake up realizing I'm not in the shape I used to be in. Step on the scale at the gym. Get ticked off at the number staring back at me and then go into hyper-crazed workout, clean-eating mode. I'm disciplined. I become a machine. Exercise is an instant obsession. I fall back in love with the sweat dripping off of me during a spin class and the muscle aches the next day after pushing myself with free weights. I crave salads. I drink protein shakes. I organize my supplements. I say no to greasy salt-bombs, and I start to feel better about myself. I keep this pace up for a while, and the pounds start to come off a little. I sense momentum and start to believe, "I can really do this. It's paying off. I CAN get back in the shape I used to be in. I see a leaner version of me in the mirror, and I like what I see." I feel more confident. I feel more me. I feel prouder of who I am and how I carry myself.

Just as I get a taste of this success and flood of positive vibes, I hit the "two-week roadblock." A full assault of temptations starts to come into my mind, like "you should reward yourself for your hard work. You deserve a burger. Wouldn't it taste amazing? C'mon Jen, one burger won't hurt you."

So, I give in to that little voice. I figure: "You know what, I DO deserve that burger. It's going to taste amazing, and I've earned it. One little burger won't hurt a thing." The burger turns into ice cream for dessert, which turns into waking up famished and going out for breakfast the next day, which becomes skipping the gym later on, which leads to adding back the weight I had just lost." The end result? A frustrated, pity-party in my mind feeling like I have to start all over again. I've flushed my hard efforts down the drain... again.

I do this because I decided to care more about the craving in that moment than I do about anything else. It's a defect I've created in my brain based on years of insecurities, growing up surrounded by comfort foods, and a feeling of constant pressure to be perfect. That was me two years ago. The version of me that didn't think I was good enough to get in better shape, that looked at myself in the mirror and grabbed areas where I was holding extra weight, that sought out my imperfections rather than actually seeing myself for what I am, and that is beautiful.

I make my downward spiral all about the burger, but the guilt I feel behind the burger wasn't about the calorie count at all. It was about something much deeper. I didn't love myself enough to commit to what was important. I learned to not trust myself or make the right decisions to continually improve myself, so instead, I chose things that took me off course. I was holding myself back because I was afraid of who I might become. I was afraid I wouldn't be accepted by the people in my life who ate poorly, never worked out, and were content with that. I was scared to be a leaner version of me when the Jen I knew always carried a little extra, even when I was a little girl. I was scared to think that people would think I'm better than them. I was scared to see what I was really capable of. I was scared to become more me, and I used my weight and eating as a mask to block me from it.

This is the enemy we all have to confront if we want to break away from mediocre and become extraordinary in our lives.

This enemy is a powerful force known as self-sabotage, and in my case, the burger was its weapon. Self-sabotage is the thing that can keep you in a cycle of stuck more than anything else, because it pulls together anything it possibly can — bad choices, negative thoughts, self-defeating beliefs — then throws them at you in one fell swoop, leaving you powerless to its force.

What makes self-sabotage so strong is that, just like my burger, it tastes great upfront, then we beat ourselves for doing it later. It creates a loop. With a behavior, we get a result. We will know what will happen as a result, so that behavior becomes a habit, when it serves us the least.

Quiet the Critic and Raise the Praise

The author Alyce Cornyn-Selby says it best, "Self-sabotage is when we say we want something and then go about making sure it doesn't happen."

It goes without saying that we are our own worst critic. The things we say in our own minds would never be things that we would openly admit, express out loud, or say to our best friend. We are harder on ourselves than we are on anyone else in our lives.

This is your biggest roadblock to achieving what you want in life. No one else can get in your way the way that you can, so understanding how self-sabotage rears its ugly head in your life will help you understand the limits you've created, so you can break past them.

It's the self-limiting beliefs that you've developed from the entire culmination of your life's experiences that are a part of what has shaped you into who you've become today. Your self-limiting beliefs provide a crutch of comfort because you are so used to thinking a certain way about yourself that you don't even realize it.

Discovering the underlying self-limiting beliefs you have takes some investigating into the depths of your mind, because they have become a habit, and habits are automatic. That's the point of a habit: It is an action you don't have to think about, similar to what we discussed around routines in the previous chapter.

With every client I work with, I see a pattern. They're not happy with their life, but they don't know why. They want to make changes, but feel paralyzed by where to start. They are so accustomed to who they have become that they can't see past the fog of their self-imposed limitations.

Breaking this pattern is paramount for you. Your 90-Day Life Challenge is a journey of change and transformation, both in how you will think and how you will act. Naturally, you may encounter unexpected roadblocks along the way, but we want to tackle the expected roadblocks. We need to disassemble the self-sabotage in your life first, otherwise, you can emerge from these 90 days the same version of who you are and wonder why you feel this way.

In fairness, I'm not saying that this is an easy process. Self-sabotage is built on years of thought patterns and behaviors that now are ingrained in you. When you strip away something you know, it can feel like you are stripping away a part of yourself. But what you are truly doing is removing what is holding you back from who you really are. As you slowly dampen the influence that self-sabotage has had in your life, you will discover what has been under the surface this whole time.

So, let's address that inner critic by first giving you some insights on why self-sabotage is in your life. Think about this for a moment: Research[8] indicates that most people speak at a rate of 150 to 200 words per minute, but the mind can listen to 450 words a minute. This means that, when you are talking to yourself, your mind is listening. It's absorbing everything you are saying to yourself and making it your reality.

The quality of your life now is directly related to the script that is playing over and over again in your mind.

Your perception of yourself is the bus that drives what you are able to do in your life, and your beliefs manifest in the way you talk to yourself. The inner voice within our minds always has something to say, and typically it's something we've been wired to say that is unkind, doubtful, and critical. It's this perception and these thoughts racing in our mind on a continual basis that influence the behaviors that you take in every moment.

If your inner voice is a critic, then you will be consumed by fear, worry, stress — and inaction.

When your self-talk is heavily critical, it leads to something I like to call the "self-sabotage loop," and it goes something like this:

- First, you have a **Limiting Thought** → You hold yourself back by your perception of yourself ("I'm not good enough.") so when you think about doing something positive, you tell yourself you can't, or you shouldn't, or you'll get to it later.

- **Excuse** → This limiting thought then opens the door for you to create an excuse for yourself to not take action on an important area of your life, because "I'm too busy. I don't have the money. It's not the right time." The excuse seems valid, because you don't want to overwhelm yourself with another task when you already have so many responsibilities. You accept that excuse as truth and use that as your voice of reason.

- **Action/Inaction** → This excuse then leads to either an action or inaction that will take you farther away from the very thing you want to do. For example, if you're telling yourself that you don't have enough time to take action on "x," you will then procrastinate and fill your time with other things that are less important.

- **Underlying Belief** → This action or inaction supports the self-limiting belief underneath all of it, which typically stems from a negative belief about yourself, such as believing that you're not good enough or worthy enough. The beliefs you have are the foundation of everything you do. They dictate your thoughts and your actions. So, any limiting thought and action can provide another supporting example for that belief. It reinforces it, giving the belief a starring role in the script you're playing in your mind.

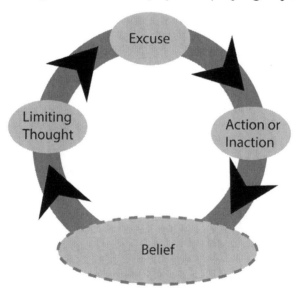

Diagram of the Self-Sabotage Loop

The self-sabotage loops force your brain to focus on the problems in your life, rather than creating solutions and momentum. With the self-sabotage loops in place, you can put off important goals and dreams in your life for weeks, months, years, even decades.

We need to start breaking these loops, so you can create urgency in your life again. The solution to getting stuck in self-sabotage loops and breaking the habits of them is by, first, mapping out what they are (like we did with your life choices in Chapter 2), and then creating a new set of beliefs and actions that will support your growth and change.

Here's what my burger self-sabotage loop looks like in the diagram:

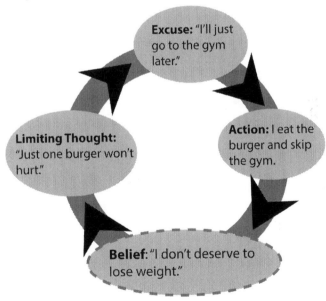

I used my belief that I didn't deserve to feel better about myself to hold me back any time I was creating momentum in my fitness goals. I got so accustomed to this belief that I made it my reality, and it kept me in a cycle of yo-yoing in my weight loss goals for years.

Two-Step Method to Breaking the Loops

The first step toward breaking self-sabotage loops is awareness and understanding of your inner critic, so you know how to quiet it. To help you tap into the self-sabotage loops you've been carrying, try this simple exercise. First, do a gut check and ask yourself:

"What is one goal I have that I can't seem to achieve, no matter what I do or how hard I try?"

I love this question because it can reveal the entire loop that's preventing you from achieving this goal Once you determine the goal, then you can look deeper:

- Think about this: What are you doing that's the opposite of your goal? What are you NOT doing to support your goal? These are your actions/inactions. For example, if you want to grow your savings, what are you doing that's affecting how much money you can put aside every month?

- I like to work backwards in the self-sabotage loop diagram by **starting with the actions first**, then the excuse, then the thought, because it is easier to observe what we are doing than it is what we are thinking. Once you know your actions and inactions, you can determine why you are doing this, which is based on your excuses and thoughts, which stems from your self-limiting belief.

- **Next, let's look at the excuses**. How are you justifying this action or inaction? Using the example around your savings, what's the excuse for spending excessively on your credit card versus stashing that money away? What are you telling yourself that you "need to" purchase, so that you avoid building up your savings instead?

- Knowing these excuses will then force you to think of why you are coming up with them. What is the **limiting thought** behind this? Typically, it comes down to something specific, like, "I'm always struggling to get by. I have to scrape to pay the bills every month."

- This limiting thought is the manifestation of a deeper belief. Once you isolate the thought(s), ask yourself, where is this coming from? Why am I thinking this? Perhaps you've told yourself that you don't deserve to have money or that money is bad or evil. Maybe at some time in your life someone told you that people with money are greedy. This belief is the crux of everything behind why you aren't accomplishing your goal, because it is talking you out of anything that can get you closer to it.

Each part of the self-sabotage loop prevents you from attaining your goal. You play through the same cycle of thoughts, excuses, and actions around and around. That's why your goal keeps looming in the distance, always seeming too far out of reach.

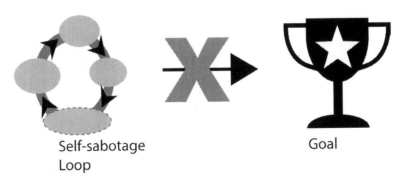

Self-sabotage
Loop

Goal

The second step to breaking self-sabotage loops is all about reframing. When you understand the deeper belief that is holding you back from achieving your goal, you can start to create a new set of beliefs that you can tell yourself.

What's really powerful about your mind is that it has the characteristic of plasticity. I'm about to get a little geeked-out on neuroscience with you here, because plasticity is the root of why you can change your beliefs at any time. So, if you're feeling a shred of doubt about your ability to break out of your self-sabotage loops, plasticity is going to be the thing that can set you free and help you see the power that you really have to control your mind and what you think.

According to BrainHQ,[9] brain plasticity — also called neuroplasticity — is an odd term for most people, with the word 'plastic' causing images of Tupperware or Saran Wrap to pop into your head. However, brain plasticity is a common term used by neuroscientists, referring to the brain's ability to change at any age."

Pay special attention to the last statement: "the brain's ability to change at any age."

What neuroscience has shown is that the brain is malleable. It's adaptive. When you give it new stimuli, it will change over time. Meaning that you can break the loops. A new stimulus can be anything from something new in your environment, like seeing a new location, to something within yourself, like a new thought.

Meaning, if you can build a new set of core beliefs, the brain will respond to those new beliefs, giving you the ability to have empowering thoughts, take decisive actions, and experience a new level of results.

What's important to recognize here is that using the power of your brain to break your self-sabotage loops isn't about just telling yourself to stop being critical or trying to block out that inner voice. You have an inner voice no matter what you say, do, or think. You can't get rid of it, so you have to retrain it.

Think about the self-limiting belief you identified in Step 1 and then complete the following statements:

1. The new belief I am going to adopt to feel positive, confident and empowered so I can achieve my goal is: _____

2. This new belief will help me accomplish: _____

3. This new belief will make me think this way about myself: _____

4. I no longer create time or space for this excuse that has held me back in the past: _____

5. I commit to take this one action that will help me achieve my goal:_____

Once you have these statements completed, now you've actually set the framework for building a new, affirming look that will propel you toward your goal, rather than sabotaging you from reaching it.

This is where plasticity comes in. You want to ingrain this new loop in your mind. You want to keep introducing this framework to your mind, so much that your brain wants to eat it for breakfast.

So, take these completed statements and put them somewhere where you can look at them every morning. Take five minutes to read these statements out loud, repeating them over and over again for the full five minutes. This exercise is like brain candy. By repeating these statements, you are creating a new loop, which will create new wiring in your brain. Remember, we crave novelty. Our brains love novelty. This is another version of it because you are giving your mind something new to think about.

This daily practice is going to feel strange at first, because your mind is used to being an inner critic. It knows the self-sabotage loops and has probably played them out more times that you care to admit.

But the more you get accustomed to this new loop and declaring these new statements, you will be more rewired to embrace this new belief, so you can think differently and act positively.

CHAPTER 7:

BRIDGING THE PRESENT GAP

"If you are depressed, you are living in the past. If you are anxious, you are living in the future. If you are at peace, you are living in the present."

— LAO ZI

THE PLACE YOU occupy in your life right now is the result of the choices you have made to get you here. The sooner you can own this, the sooner you will feel free to create your life, rather than wait for it to happen.

Now as I write this, I'm mindful that things do happen to us. There are things we experience that are out of our control. I've been fired and didn't choose it. I've lost loved ones and definitely didn't choose that. I've been mistreated and misunderstood and didn't want that.

But if we focus on the things that have happened to us, rather than what we do and how we react to those things in the now, we will end up as a passive bystander in our lives, just waiting for more things to happen and hoping that more good than bad things will come into our lives.

On the opposite side of this is the focus of this chapter, and that is:

Master how to play an active role in the course of your life, so you can own your choices from the past and look ahead to where you are going to create your future, but most importantly, *focus on the present*.

If you feel like you have been a spectator in your life, you are probably getting stuck in something that I like to call "the present gap."

When someone is caught in the present gap, they end up doing one of two things consistently:

1. They spend time looking back in the past and wishing to go back to times gone by, or they look back to the past with regrets, questioning their decisions. This is especially common if someone finds themselves in a place in life that they are unhappy with.

2. Then they look to the future, in hopes that in time things will get better. They hope their money, health, love, and life situation will change "all in good time."

When someone is stuck in the present gap, it's easy to feel frustrated in the present and the current circumstances they're surrounded by, wishing for things they want to have or used to have.

Here's how I define the present gap:

Getting lost in the past or the future, without seeing the present moment.

The moment you are experiencing right now is the most important moment of your life, because it's this very moment that you can control and change.

You can't change the past and you can't predict the future, but if you focus on the present, you will feel more control in your life now — and where you are headed.

Minimizing Your "What-Ifs"

What keeps people stuck in the present gap are the "what if" questions. As humans, we're naturally curious. If you think back to that time as a child, you always questioned things. You were on a constant journey to develop, grow, and learn. Everything felt new because everything was new, so naturally you wanted to question more and understand more.

Curiosity is a good thing. It keeps us hungry to learn and challenge our core beliefs and what we know to be true.

Questioning ourselves, though, should not be misconstrued as being the same thing as curiosity. If we over-question ourselves, we can create that "life hamster wheel," where you feel like you're just spinning around doing the same thing.

Over-questioning leads to doubt, uncertainty, and opens the door to fear. In fact, getting too curious can lead to feeling like you're banging your head against the wall not knowing what to do next in your life.

I will challenge you in this section to really ask yourself: "Am I being curious or am I over-questioning myself?" I'm going to help you understand what the difference is and how to tip the scales towards curiosity, because that is what will help you stay in the present and reflect on your life right now.

So first, let's look at the habit of over-questioning. If you're wondering why you aren't moving ahead in life, then it's likely because you are "what-iffing yourself" into a corner.

People can "what if" the past...

- What if I should've done this?
- What if I had made this decision instead?
- What if the decision I made was wrong?
- What if I said yes to this? What if I said no?

All these questions do is mull a time gone by and wonder how differently your life would be now if you had done something different. You can glean power from that type of hindsight, if it helps you understand the lessons learned and make better decisions in the future (which is what we discussed in Chapter 3). But there is a difference between staying stuck in looking to the past for answers rather than using such reflection as a tool for growth.

People can also "what if" the future and get caught in overthinking the next step in their lives, so much so that it stops them in their tracks.

- What if I try this and I fail?
- What if I make a decision and I wake up in a few years not happy?

- What if my success is short-lived?
- What if someone else has the same idea?
- What if my idea isn't good enough to work?
- What if I get told no?

The common thing behind all of these questions is the fear that what you choose won't work and that you will fail. Here's what is interesting about how people commonly think through these types of questions: The "what-ifs" become the scapegoat. They usually lead to people thinking about the negative consequences of the decisions they've made in the past, and overlay that vision onto the decisions they want to make in the future. Furthermore, they tend to also seek out the positive consequences of the decisions they wish they had made in the past. They put themselves between a rock and a hard place, not knowing where to go next, paralyzed by thinking that their previous decisions were wrong and that a different decision would have been so much better.

This train of thought can keep you stuck in a cycle of doubting yourself so much that you choose to not make any forward movement at all, because you're allowing the past to question your future.

That was Tricia. She was caught in a whirlwind of so much what-iffing that her business had been stagnant for two years. At the rate she was going, Tricia would end up having to fold on her dreams and find a job because she was barely able to keep up with her monthly overhead.

Despite the hamster wheel that she and her business were on, Tricia also knew what she wanted. She was a passionate doctor, with a drive to truly change the lives of the people in her community. She adored working with athletes, because she felt a sense of purpose in helping them prevent injuries and elevate their performance to the next level. Tricia was also incredible at what she did. Her patients ranged from triathletes to weekend warriors, and she loved the challenge of customizing her care to a level of surgical precision for what each patient needed. That is why her patients got results.

At the time she hired me as a coach, Tricia was on the brink of walking away from it all, even though that's not what she wanted. She came to me in a moment of crisis, wondering how she could still be stuck in the same place and never able to get ahead. She wasn't getting referrals. Her patient visits were the same week after week. She wasn't growing, and her profits were getting dumped back into keeping her practice afloat.

I knew that I had to establish a baseline with her while also getting a sense for what her vision for her business really was. In my experience, the heart of every business owner is impact. What they care most about is how can they influence and serve people. They are driven by how they can make a big contribution and change the lives of others.

So that was our starting point, and I asked Tricia to outline for me, with the same precision she uses in her treatment plans, what her 3-year business plan looks like and how she wants to get there.

Now here's where this gets really fascinating...

Tricia gave me one of the clearest visions I had seen from any of my clients ever. Typically, I'll find that a client doesn't even know what their vision is because they have gotten so bogged down by the trappings of "shoulds," routines, doubts, and conventional thinking. But Tricia actually knew what she wanted. She knew that she wanted to be seen as a thought leader in her community. She envisioned being the go-to expert for her community and sharing her knowledge through speaking engagements and lectures. She also knew she wanted to elevate her impact and that, once her practice was booked, she wanted to expand her offerings through online programs and books so she could reach more people outside of her community.

So how is it that this lively, engaging woman knew what she wanted but couldn't get there?

I knew that somehow she was lost in the present gap. She was caught up on what happened in her past, or what could happen in her future. Because when I drilled down to ask her what she had done in the past three months to get her business steered in the direction of her vision, she hung her head down sheepishly. She admitted to me: "I've been hiding. I've been doing a bunch of busywork but not doing what I really should be doing. I haven't done anything to market my practice at all."

So, I called out the irony and asked her to reflect more: "What is making you want to hide when you know what it is that you want?"

And the doors flooded open to Tricia's "what-if" list:

- "I don't think I'm ready yet."

- "I need more training and certifications that I should have done in school but didn't."

- "There's another doctor in this area that is so much more qualified than me and everyone loves her. I just don't know why people would want to see me instead of her."

- "I don't know if people will like the topics I want to share."

- "I don't think people are ready to hear my message."

- "What if this doesn't work?"

- "What if I have a patient that I don't know how to take care of?"

- "What if my husband has to keep working enough to support both of us, not matter how hard I try?"

- "What if I end up moving out of the area some day?"

Tricia was what-iffing herself out of doing anything. She what-iffed her impact. She what-iffed her value. She didn't think she was qualified enough. She didn't think she was good enough, and she what-iffed herself into a box of indecision.

Tricia's clarity was there. It had been there the whole time, *but her conviction was missing.* Her questions weren't serving her to assess and act, they were forcing her to doubt and sit.

Because Tricia questioned the decisions she had previously made, such as not getting more certifications to her already extensive list, she was less compelled to act on getting herself out into the community more. Because she questioned her magnetism and ability to attract opportunities, Tricia focused on the failures of what *could* go wrong, rather than see the potential that her business vision had.

The "what-ifs" make you feel completely dis-empowered, because you criticize your own decisions and think the decisions you didn't make might have been better. And this makes you question your ability to make a good decision for your future.

It's a battle between the past and your future, without reflecting on the here and now and completely owning your choices.

Part of creating a 90-Day Life Challenge is to help you stop questioning what you do, what you did, or what you could do, and just go for it. To get intuitive again. Listen to what your gut or heart or soul wants in this moment and run with it. To dive into life with the same curiosity and fearlessness that you did as a child. To own the choices you have made that have brought you to this point, and take advantage of the moment here right now.

You've gotta bring back that hunger and start breaking the "what-if" loops, just like we did with self-sabotage, so you can let go of your past and stop worrying about your future.

Because in the end, what will matter to you the most is that you went for it.

So, before creating your own 90-Day Life Challenge, we have to address how to handle the what-if loops, because they *will* show up. I'm making a safe bet that you've dealt with them in your own life up to this point.

So, here's my two-step approach to not only break the "what-ifs" of the past, but rewire them in your brain:

Again, this is preliminary work before you kick off your challenge. The work we put into this now will set the stage for creating a new version of your life.

1. The first step is look back on the past decisions you have made in your life. I'm talking about the decisions that you question to this day.

    Your default will be to look to the reasons why it was a bad decision, but the challenge here is to actually look at how this decision has actually served you.

    Think of one decision in your past that you keep replaying in your mind or going back to during pivotal points when you're planning to make a big decision.

    Just start with one so you can apply this process, and then you can then repeat it with other past decisions. Ask yourself these two questions: What was that past decision, and what are positive lessons that you can glean from it?

I'll give you an example. When I moved to Washington, D.C., in 2007 to start my career as a chiropractor, never in my life did I imagine that I would end up there. I'm from the Midwest and if my heart was pulling me anywhere, it wasn't the East Coast. Six months prior to moving to D.C., I did a four-month residency in New Zealand, where I made a ton of friends, played in the outdoors, explored the country, had a great work-life balance, and felt like I was home.

So, when I returned to the States, I was set on moving to the West Coast, where there are mountains, coastlines, and national parks anywhere within a day's drive. But despite my efforts, I couldn't land a job, so when I threw a dart and applied to work in a practice in Washington, I got the job right away and figured that was a sign that I was supposed to be there.

For the next seven years, I questioned my decision. It was a fast-paced, high-stress, concrete jungle. My heart kept calling me out west, but I now had commitments that kept me stuck from having the courage to move.

I initially looked back at that period of my life with regret. I would tell myself that I "wasted so much time living in a place that I never wanted to be in in the first place." I would berate myself asking, "What if had just packed up and headed west and figured it out? What if I wasn't so scared? What if I didn't sacrifice my lifestyle for my career?"

But if I had stayed in that headspace, I would've been lost in a sea of building regret that would've just accumulated over time. Instead, I had a flip of perspective and realized something huge from that one decision. My time in D.C. gave me clarity. I became hyper-aware of what I didn't want and what was at the root of my unhappiness. I grew to understand the type of lifestyle I wanted and what was important to me in my life, which led me to consider:

OK, if this wasn't what I wanted, then what is it that I do want? What makes me happy? How do I get there? What do I do first? Once I understood the qualities in life that made me happy, it helped me determine what decisions to make, so I had more of that in my life. As a surprise bonus, looking at this what-if from my past became a gift of appreciation, because now I appreciate even more living in areas that I love and having the freedom to travel, so much more now than I would have had if it had just come easy to me back in my 20s and I had made a different decision then.

My what-if became my clarity. What was once a source of lament, now became a source of gratitude.

2. That's the root of the next step in breaking away from wasting time what-iffing the past. What do you have in your life now because of the lessons you've learned from that past decision? What can you be grateful for because of it? How can you look at decisions from your past and see them as a gift?

Play Out the Fears

"I learned that courage was not the absence of fear, but the triumph over it. The brave man is not he who does not feel afraid, but he who conquers that fear."

— **NELSON MANDELA**

Fear. We all face it. We all deal with it, most times on a daily basis. It's in our wiring. Our primal brains want to seek out fears to keep us alive. We are designed to look for the dangers in our environment, so we can defend ourselves against them.

That wiring doesn't serve us when the thing we are trying to defend against is ourselves. It just keeps us stuck. What our brains do really well, all too well, is create the "what-if" fears of the future.

And that's the biggest roadblock to people taking action in their own lives and living into their potential. You must look under the surface at what fears have been holding you back, so you know how to crush them.

Your fears are the foundation of all self-sabotage loops, excuses, inaction, and procrastination.

Fear is the reason why Tricia was in the position she was in. She had let fears dominate her life, so much that she wasn't focusing on the things that could propel change. Instead, she was hiding in useless busywork hoping that would comfort her enough to make her feel busy and productive.

Facing Your Fear of Failure

If we were to take any dream you have in your own life that you've been putting on hold, the root of it will almost always come down to the fear of failure. It's that little voice in your subconscious brain that is telling you, "what if you fail?" The voice is quiet but powerful. It's nagging and it's incessant.

While the fear of failure is there to protect us, it can also trap us, which is why we need to look at it head on and understand it. Play with it. Grow to accept it and utilize it, rather than try to ignore it or hate ourselves for having it, because it's a part of who we are.

This fear keeps you in a cycle of wishing, wanting, and hoping, rather than doing. It also keeps you comfortable. It's why it took me over a year to start writing this book. I was scared it would suck. People wouldn't like it. People wouldn't get it. People wouldn't like me.

The fear of failure is why so many people are burned out of work, life, and love, but stay where they are. Your "what-ifs" about the future push you back to your comfort zone, because it's easier to feel safe and comfortable doing what you know than it is to push yourself to try something new.

Fear creates resistance. It creates the strongest barrier that we cannot see, but we feel at the core of our beings. Fear is our mind's way of telling us, "Don't try and risk it. It's safer where you are right now."

**But if you're not happy with where
you are in life right now, then
you are just letting fear win.**

Not only can fear erect a barrier within our minds, we're also fed the idea that change is scary. Rarely are we encouraged to see that change can actually be liberating. So, we don't allow our minds to go there. We avoid change because we're afraid that change can lead to failure, rather than create a space to see how those changes can create the fulfillment we truly seek.

But no matter how much change is feared, it will happen regardless. We'll get older. The years will fly by. Opportunities in our life will appear and vanish. Change will happen whether we do anything or not, so why not embrace change.

Remember, we inherently crave novelty, and novelty is the foundation of creating change. Novelty makes us happier and more fulfilled, so it's better if we actually sit in the driver's seat of change rather than wait for it to happen.

It is in the changes you're courageous to make where you'll find out who you can really become.

Tricia wasn't happy, but her unhappiness wasn't enough motivation for her to overcome her fears. Her unhappiness was the comfort that clouded her courage. She needed to find a way to actually face her fears rather than just accept them.

For Tricia, her biggest fear was that her business would fail, and she wouldn't gain the respect and impact she desired. Even when she was already faced with that reality, this fear kept driving her back to square 1. I knew Tricia had to look at this fear from a different lens, so she wouldn't just identify with it. She had to see the pain that choosing fear would create in her life, not just now, but in the future.

> *"Tricia, tell me something, what will your practice look like five years down the road if you keep doing the same thing?" I asked.*

"I don't think I'll have a practice if I keep up this pace," she admitted. "I'm not seeing enough patients and not making enough money. It already isn't working."

In that instant, I felt the need to hold up the mirror to Tricia and show her what she needed to see. "Then, isn't it safe to say you are already failing, so what do you have to lose?"

I'm just going to call this out right now: If you are afraid that you're going to fail at something, it's probably because you are failing anyway.

- If you're afraid you won't lose the extra weight, then aren't you already failing because you aren't as healthy as you want to be?

- If you're too afraid to start your own business, then you probably want to do your own thing because you are miserable in your job and failing to live with purpose.

- If you're afraid to end a relationship because you don't want to be alone, then you are already failing to be good to yourself.

What most people don't realize is that the fear of failure projects into the future a reflection of a failure that is currently happening in the present.

I know this may seem harsh, but I'm not going to give you some rose-colored view on this. I've witnessed far too many people who have let fear paralyze them for the entire course of their lives. They focus on what could go wrong rather than what could go right.

This is why we need to get visceral. I need you to see what this fear is doing to you now, and how it is setting the course for your future, a future you have been afraid to change.

Overcoming the fear of failure is deceptively simple. More simple than you have been taught to believe. This goes back to the power of predicting your regrets that we discussed in Section 1 and feeling them. I want you to feel the impact of living into your fears so visually that you actually fear the fear.

Harnessing the Power of Fear

Only by facing the fear can you strip it of its power. Because if you can play out what your life is like if you let whatever fear of failure stay in control, you will be more motivated to act against it and actually see that there is nothing to fear at all.

Consider these questions and how they relate to your own fears:

1. What is a fear of failure that you currently face? What are the "what-if" statements you are saying to yourself to reinforce that fear?

2. How is it controlling your life right now?

3. What it is preventing you from doing? What's the goal underneath the fear?

4. What will your life look like in 5, 10, 20 years if you continue to succumb to this fear?

I also recognize the fact that just going through these questions doesn't erase the potential that you could actually fail. Things might not actually go the way you expect, but that doesn't mean you shouldn't act on a decision because of it, which is why I'm going to ask that you consider these questions as well:

5. Play out the "what-ifs." Play out the fear and the failure. What happens if the worst-case scenario you are crafting in your brain really does come to pass?

6. What obstacles could you face along the way? How could you get around them? Anticipate the potential challenges you may face and create a plan to solve them. Plot out any obstacle you can imagine that can crop up, block you, or trip you up, so you know how to dodge it.

7. If you did actually fail and that fear really came true after all, what action would you take? What would you do to course-correct your life if you made the wrong move, the wrong choice of job, partner, location, you name it?

You'd find a way to figure it out, right? You wouldn't just want to stay in a place of failing. You'd want to break free of it. You'd have to find a way out of it.

When you can both play out how the fear of failure is holding you back, as well as what you would actually do if the worst-case scenario materialized and that fear came true, it no longer has power over you.

So, work through these questions and create the action plan to counter your fear of failure. Give yourself the opportunity to control where a decision can take you, rather than play the game of blaming life or being a victim to what could go wrong.

And if you can do this, you will be able to reset your ability to make decisions in your own life, with a renewed sense of inner power, and actually go for it.

Because then you can start to use "what-ifs" as a source of motivation and as a planning tool, and focus on what you are doing in the present moment to make them happen.

This is what will help you create a 90-Day Life Challenge that can completely change the course of who you are, and finally liberate you from those fears and "what-if" loops that have been keeping you in the cycle of stuck.

Projecting your fear of failure into the future is no small feat. Be gentle with yourself as you answer these questions, and remember that this is designed to help you no longer live into your fears, but actually *have the courage to act despite them*. You have the power to change how you use this fear and channel it as a source of motivation, so you can address what it is about your present life that you want to change.

This is a difficult exercise, I know. I've looked back on the past five years of being unhappy with my fat, finances, and friends. When I played that out another five years, I didn't like what I saw and that was my catalyst to change.

The answers you find will actually be the key to help you transform fear of failure into the fear of not trying. You will recognize that there is no choice other than to act, because you would rather try than expect you'll fail.

Here's how you switch from the fear of failure to the fear of not trying:

1. Think about that goal you have hiding underneath the fear of failure.

2. What will you miss out on if you don't try? What could your life look like if you accomplished it?

Another way to look at this is to think of positive "what-if" statements that reinforce the achievement of this goal.

- *What if I can create exactly what I want?*
- *What if I can accomplish this goal?*
- *What if this really worked?*
- *What if I did lose the weight?*
- *What if my new business skyrockets?*
- *What if I find a partner who brings out the best in me?*

It's this level of awareness that gave Tricia the courage to act. She no longer filled her days with busywork. Instead, she found meaning in what she did every day. She looked to her business plan that had been there all this time and asked the "what-ifs" in a positive light.

She took the courage to put herself out there, build new relationships, and seek out opportunities to educate people in her community.

Was she afraid to do all of this? Of course. But was she more afraid of not making a go of it to create the business she deserved? You better believe it.

CHAPTER 8:

THE ART OF GETTING SELFISH

*"You must make your dream a priority
in order for it to become your life."*

— BOB PROCTOR

FEARS ALLOW US to get lost in our own head and get in our own way, and what often happens is that these fears actually cause us to put ourselves last. Our desires get masked by our insecurities. Our wants get masked by our responsibilities. Our goals get masked by our demands.

We can forget ourselves along the way because of things outside of us, be they circumstances, our current situation, and others' needs from us. The longer we keep this up, the more likely that we will at some point realize we have proverbially "let ourselves go."

This chapter is going to redefine how you think about yourself as a priority in your own life. There are core questions that we need to ask to fuel us to become better versions of ourselves, like, "What's missing in my life? What do I want? What do I really *need*? What's important to me?"

We are not the culmination of the people or things in our lives, though it's easy to define ourselves based on what's outside of us because it's what we can see. What we truly are, though, is based on the depth of how much we are living into the authentic version of ourselves and then putting this version out into the world.

Who are you, *really?* If you had to define yourself right now, what would you base your answer on? Do you know who that is? Have you given yourself the chance to understand who you really are? I'm talking about the version of you that cannot wait to get out of bed in the morning. The person who feels "on" every day and is genuinely happy.

I want to introduce a concept that is going to sound contradictory for a moment, but roll with me...

To live into your potential and have an extraordinary life, you have to get selfish.

You have to put yourself first. This is actually a good thing, but the world tells us that it's not. By selfish I don't mean that you are egocentric, self-serving, inconsiderate, narcissistic, mean-spirited, and downright petty. And I'm certainly not suggesting that you get so lost in what you want and need that you forget others and lose your sense of compassion.

That's the classic definition of selfish and the ugly kind of selfish. The kind that steers people away from you and leads to a miserable existence.

I'm going to flip the definition of selfish on its head and introduce you to the good, loving, uplifting, soul-nourishing, life-fulfilling, move mountains kind of selfish.

When people put themselves last in life, they think they are doing everyone a favor, including themselves, because they focus on others' needs and get stuff done. They're typically seen as highly productive and are greatly appreciated by the people in their life. Their loved ones know them as a compassionate and giving person, the kind that would give the shirt off their back.

Again, these qualities are beautiful. I believe we live in a time where compassion toward others is more important than it has ever been. The social graces of saying good morning, opening the door for others, and thanking someone are becoming a lost art. I believe our society is driving the bus on instant gratification and self-validation, as opposed to loving unconditionally.

Here is the distinction that I'm going to point out:

You can only go on so long putting other's needs before your own. Love is what makes the world go around, but at the foundation of that is self-love. How are you treating yourself? What are you doing to create and sustain internal joy? How are you satisfying your own needs? Do you love who you are, how you spend your time, and the direction your life is going?

If the end-result of how you live is that you put your needs last, you will never be able to create any time or energy for you.

Obviously, the people in your life have needs. Your partner, parents, children, friends, coworkers, community, clients, and customers, among others. But so do you. If you have an imbalance between your needs and others' needs, it's probably leading to things in your life like anxiety, resentment, sadness, fatigue, frustration, irritability, among others. You may not recognize why these emotions are there or you try to channel these emotions to smaller nuances of day-to-day life, like getting into a fight over taking out the garbage or doing the dishes, but that's just a projection. You're just channeling those emotions there, because it's safer to do that than it is to channel them toward what is really going on, which is that you are neglecting something that is important to you.

It is my goal in this chapter to help you discover what that is, and when you do, your priorities and dreams will become clearer, so you'll have the framework you need to do your 90-Day Life Challenge, which we'll map out in Section 3.

All these feelings, by the way, indicate a deeper need within you and are the classic signs of life burnout.[10]

Getting selfish (in a good way) is about creating self-love again. To start to listen to what your mind, heart, and being have been trying to tell you about what they need for a long time, and to not let that part of you go quiet. This is about putting yourself first again, or maybe doing it for the first time in your life. By the way, the end-result of incorporating this type of selfishness is that you will be better equipped to not only tend to yourself, but love and support the people in your life. It's a win-win.

Practicing Selfishness

To learn the art of putting yourself again, you have to break this down into three simple steps:

1. You need to ask yourself: What are the things that distract you from your own needs on a regular basis? I like to think of these as the **distractors** in your life. Where is your energy getting pulled in ways that actually don't benefit you? It could be things like spending too much time on email or social media, getting frustrated watching the news, constantly trying to uplift a needy friend, putting toxic foods into your body, or having regular negative thoughts dominating your mind. Walk yourself through a given day and think about the things you are doing that are NOT taking you closer to your goals. Think about the things that you say "yes" to because you feel obligated, but if you think on it deeper, you wish you would say, "no." Where do you over-commit yourself?

   You need to understand and reassess the things in your life that are taking up your energy that are not serving you. Go back to the routine-flushing work we did in Chapter 4 and see if anything on that list pops out as something that isn't necessary at all, and just drains your precious time.

2. Start to look at the things that you want or wish you could be doing in any given day, week, or month but put on hold because you're telling yourself

things like, "I'm too busy. I don't have enough time. It'll have to wait."

These are the things you know that, if you put more time and focus on regularly, you'd be happier because of them. I like to call these the **self-shifters**, because they will tip the scales to putting your needs first. But you currently deny yourself this pleasure because you've allowed other responsibilities, priorities, and distractions to stop you from doing these things and putting them first. Think about how you want to be spending your free time, such as engaging in new hobbies. These could be things like going to the gym, making dinner rather than going out to eat, having a weekend with your friends, going to the spa, or taking your bike out for a ride.

3. Look at that list of things in #2 and rank them, then direct your attention to the top item on your list. Put all your attention there and ask yourself, "what is one small step I can take right now to incorporate this into my life *today*?"

I'll give you an example of this 3-step process in action to illustrate how powerful this can be to peel away the layers of who you are now to who you want to become and why getting selfish is a very beautiful thing.

I had a coaching client, Callie, who was in a transition of getting ready to leave a job she had been in for five years to start her own practice. She was afraid of making the change, but she knew she couldn't take the pressures of the work schedule, demands, and low pay any more.

She also knew she would be much more successful and have much more freedom if she was doing her own thing and being her own boss.

But Callie's biggest challenge was that she kept telling herself that she just didn't "have enough time." She didn't have enough free time. She didn't have enough time to sleep. She didn't have enough time to spend with her husband. She didn't have enough time to work on her business plans.

She. Just. Didn't. Have. Enough. Time.

In fairness, Callie's schedule was off-the-charts crazy. She was working six days a week at her current job and clocking in 60 hours easy. Having been in a similar position myself, I know how much more constrained time can feel working at that pace.

But Callie's first roadblock was how ingrained the story of "I don't have enough time" was in her internal dialogue. It was her way of life, and she owned it to her detriment. What did this story create for her? Well for starters, Callie was exhausted, frazzled, and stressed from the demands of her job. She would come home at night and, rather than spend time with her husband or enjoy free time to herself, she would collapse in bed just to wake up the next morning then rinse and repeat the same routine all over again. Any spare time she did have was focused on tending to things in and around the house, leaving no room for her hobbies, let alone her ambitions. She was being completely selfless and felt like she had no choice in the matter.

In fact, Callie told me that she hadn't been herself in years. The last time she said she truly felt like the free-spirited, fun-loving person she used to be was back in college, which was almost 10 years ago at the time.

I saw the imbalance right away. She was wired to give to others. She's a nurturer at heart, in addition to being a free spirit. She devoted her life and career to helping others, so naturally it was her default to focus on the needs of the people in her life first. Combine that default with the scarcity of time she felt, and she was doomed to have no chance to put herself first.

So, when I introduced the concept of being selfish to Callie, it felt very foreign to her, and she resisted it at first, telling me, "I can't focus on myself now. I don't have the time. When I have my own practice, I'll have the freedom to focus on me again."

"But Callie, if you don't open up the time to put yourself first now, then you can't create the space to do your own thing, including time to focus on building your business. If you can't build your business, then you'll stay exactly where you are. I don't know about you, but that doesn't sound very free-spirited to me," I replied.

I was poking a hole in her argument and she knew it. She knew that the crux of her not feeling free-spirited was because of the mental trap she created for herself. She built this idea of hoping that, by being amazing at taking care of everything and everyone else, she would find enough satisfaction.

I challenged her to look past how she was living her life now and told her that, if she wanted to bridge the gap of currently feeling consumed by her job and working towards experiencing the freedom of being her own boss, she needed to start to redefine how she perceived her time.

In following this 3-step framework, we first looked at where she was spending her time that wasn't helping her cause. What Callie discovered was that she was wasting more time than she realized on the distractors, like watching TV, mindlessly scrolling through email and Facebook, spending hours on chores around the house that she admittedly could spend less time on. All these distractors were just habits and a part of her daily routine. She didn't see them as time-wasters because she just did them without conscious thought.

Then we looked at rediscovering the things she really wanted to do in her free time, and I asked her, "if you could bring one thing into your life starting today, just one thing that would bring you more happiness, what would that be?"

"Yoga," she replied in an instant. "I used to do yoga back in college, and I absolutely loved it."

Isn't it ironic that she was doing something she loved at a time in her life when she felt the most authentic and free?

Yoga was her self-shifter.

So I asked her, "If you brought yoga back into your life, how would you feel differently from how you do now?"

"Oh, I would be so much happier. I'd feel more calm and confident. I think I would actually feel better at work and my patients wouldn't see me as stressed anymore. I could focus more on taking care of them. I'd probably be better for my husband, and probably a lot more fun to hang out with when I'm with my friends..."

The list of benefits was just pouring out of her, so it begged the question that I had to ask next, "Then why aren't you doing it?"

"Well it was easier to do yoga in college. I had friends and we could go to classes together. Now I'm in a place where I don't really know anybody, and I'd feel uncomfortable going to a class alone. It's kind of cliquey here in this community, so I'm not sure I'd feel welcome. I mean I guess I could do yoga at home, but I have a dog, so I'd have to talk to my husband to see if he could make sure the dog doesn't distract me while I do yoga. Plus, there's not much space in our house. I don't really have a space that's just for yoga. There's so much clutter and stuff around..."

What makes this response so interesting is that she was creating her own barriers and excuses for not doing yoga, the very thing that she already knew would bring more joy to her life. She was focusing on the minor obstacles blocking her from doing it, rather than seeing the problems and creating solutions to them. She didn't give herself the time or space to do something that was inherently so important to her, because she was accustomed to putting up walls for herself so she could open the door for others.

She got so used to being trapped by the makings and stories of her current life — not enough time, a frustrating job, and feeling stressed — that she gave up her power to put herself first and focus on what she needs.

Even though, deep down, Callie knew that putting yoga back into her life would actually create so many benefits.

So, we started to look at how she could start to get selfish again. In other words, how could she put more focus on herself, self-love, and what's important to her.

This leads to the third step of practicing selfishness, which again is, think about one priority you want to bring into your life (again something that would bring more joy), and creating one tiny step you could take to start to make that happen.

For my client, I knew I had to make this simple. I knew I couldn't encourage her to drop everything and go on a yoga retreat for a week. I had to help her create a small win for herself. All I wanted to help her see right now was one small action she could take, and that's how I set the stage. With the pressure off the table, Callie started to ponder what she could do and starting thinking out loud... "I guess I could just set up a small space to put down my yoga mat in my house, then let my husband know that I'd like a few minutes of quiet time to do yoga."

And there it was, her solution. Callie found her own answer just by giving herself a moment to go beyond the excuses and the stories, and just *listen within.*

As a coach, I'm also an accountability partner. I make sure that my clients don't just say they're going to do something, but that they actually commit to themselves that they're going to do it. It takes tangible action steps and deadlines to move forward in life, so to seal the deal with a little accountability and make sure Callie started to act on this, I had to ask one more question: "How soon can you commit to doing this?"

"Today," she replied, without hesitation.

Fast-forward 30 days — Callie had focused on practicing yoga for 5-10 minutes a day in the comfort of her home, and she found herself happier, lighter, and more at peace in her life, even with the current circumstances that used to make her miserable. Her husband, friends, and coworkers found her more enjoyable to be around. She even enjoyed her work more, and her patients saw a brighter, more vibrant Callie. Even her boss took notice.

Interesting isn't it? Even though her circumstances didn't change, her happiness grew because she shifted her priorities. Imagine now what the happier version of Callie can do to launch her business. Plus, look at the domino effect of good that happened to Callie just by bringing one thing that was important to her back into her life.

So, let's look at what this could look like for you. Now that you know the 3-steps of practicing selfishness, go back to that one thing at the top of your list that will give an instant dose of joy to your life and ask yourself this:

- What benefits would you experience by making this a priority? How would you feel? How would that impact your energy and outlook on life?

- That's just looking at changing one thing, I might add. Imagine a day-to-day life where you focused on your entire set of core needs. How would your life look and feel different compared to what it is now? This, by the way, is going to be one of the core objectives of your 90-Day Life Challenge.

- How would the people in your life benefit if they got to experience a happier, more fulfilled you?

This third question is so important because being selfish actually allows you to put more energy into the people, work, and causes you care about. By putting more focus on your needs and wants, you can nurture yourself and have more energy to focus on other people in your life that you love and support. The people in your life benefit by your newfound selfishness.

You become more you. They get to experience more of the awesome you. You feel more alert, energized, confident.

Self-Limiting Definitions

"Limits, like fears, are often just an illusion."

— MICHAEL JORDAN

You can see in Callie how she was putting self-imposed limits on herself. Through a combination of her self-sabotage loops, fears, and unselfishness, she had trapped herself into a way of life that wasn't making her happy.

These limits were a fog for her, clouding her from being the free-spirit she really was and reaching the goals she had set out for herself. She couldn't see past them, for they were defining her. She saw herself as a woman who had no free will, succumbing to the circumstances surrounding her.

This is what I refer to as a "self-limiting definition:" Defining yourself by your circumstances and the limits you place on yourself because of those circumstances.

> *Callie's self-limiting definition was, "I don't have time to work on my business, therefore I will never be able to have my own business."*

Self-limiting definitions cause you to avoid the dreams you want to pursue because you allow yourself to think that the idea is too grand, complex, expensive, far-reaching, or difficult to achieve. This is why people end up in a position where they put their own needs last because they tell themselves that it's impossible for them to fulfill their own needs, so they might as well focus on the needs of others.

Note that, at this stage, we are looking at the core of who you are. When we mapped out your self-sabotage loops and fears in previous chapters, that was designed so you could look at what is happening on the surface — the thoughts, behaviors, and actions you could observe that are holding you back in life.

We did this to start to peel away the layers of limitation, one at a time, like the layers of onion. Starting with the surface layers that are thinner and easier to pull away, now we are getting deeper, so you can understand how you are defining yourself, how that is preventing you from what you want, and redefine what's important to you.

Only by addressing the limits of what you believe you can do, despite your current circumstances, are you able to create a transformation in your life. Self-limiting definitions do just that. They mask your priorities and put up barriers, so you can't focus on what's important for you or act on it.

I know we're covering a lot of ground in this chapter, but this is a fundamental stage of your journey. I've had clients tell me that this type of evaluation was the catalyst to changing their lives and helping them break out of the same situation they had been stuck in for years. I want you to really dig deep here, because we're going to look at the limitations you are imposing upon yourself, then we're going to strip them away, so you can reassess your priorities in life.

Knowing your limitations will help you determine what is missing. What is missing will bring out the goals you've had all this time, but hidden from. Those goals will be the framework for your 90-Day Life Challenge.

I'm going to share with you a set of statements that will prompt you to peel away your own layers and discover what you have been hiding.

Complete the following statements:

1. I have been holding myself back from doing _____
   _____.

2. This has limited me from becoming
   _____. Think about the person
   you will be by doing what you have been putting
   on hold.

3. The reason I have been holding myself back is _____
   _____. Here, think about
   the story you are telling yourself. What excuses do
   you keep creating? What barriers do you put in your
   way? This reason is the basis of your self-limiting
   definition.

   Maybe you want to go to the beach every week, but
   feel too self-conscious in a swimsuit and want to
   wait until you get all the extra weight off.

   Maybe you want to go on some extreme
   backpacking expedition, but you tell yourself you
   can't because you have priorities like your job and
   family and just don't have the means.

   Maybe you want to have more friends in your life,
   but you don't go out to meet more people.

   Maybe you want to have more money and
   abundance, but you haven't mustered up the
   courage to ask for a promotion or a raise.

4. If I replaced my excuses with action, the first action
   I would take is _____?

5. I would define my authentic self as someone who is _____. If you're struggling with this statement, think of a time in your life when you were in total bliss. Who were you at that time? How would you describe that version of you?

6. From that definition, write out the top three qualities that describe you at your best. This will be the foundation of re-establishing your priorities in life, which we will address next.

Priorities of the Present

"The key is not to prioritize what's on your schedule, but to schedule your priorities."

— **STEVEN COVEY**

The quality of your life is based on the priorities of your life.

For so many people, their mind is like a cluttered house, constantly sorting out all the different things that they must do. It's a constant mental ping-pong of bouncing around from one item on the list to the next, feeling compelled to keep trudging on until everything on that list is scratched off, but the list never goes away.

People think they are staying accountable to their priorities, but they are only staying stuck in their to-dos. They aren't living into their authentic self. Their priorities have been long forgotten and replaced by jam-packed schedules. This is not a life of quality. This is a life of commitments and obligations. There is no room for the qualities most important to you, if you aren't making the time for them.

When you think of the three qualities that describe you at your best, ask yourself, "how well am I living into those priorities?"

- Does your lifestyle reflect those qualities?
- Do the people in your life support those qualities or diminish them?
- Are the choices you're making on a day-to-day basis supporting those qualities?

If you've answered "no" to any or all of these questions, then there is a gap between the quality of your life and the priorities you are making in your life.

Our goal in creating your 90-Day Life Challenge will be to help you live into those qualities as much as possible by prioritizing what you do and what you focus on, and I'm guessing that, by the work we're doing in this section of the book, you're recognizing that you have let these qualities slide.

I'll give you a personal example of the gap I experienced and what I had to change in my life.

For me, my three qualities are:

- FREEDOM
- JOY
- PASSION

I had a wake-up call in my life when I wasn't experiencing these qualities at all. I had hit my own wall of obligations and attachments that left me feeling stuck, unhappy, and stagnant. Quite the opposite of who I am when I feel genuinely happy.

So, I had to ask myself a few things: "What do each of these qualities mean to me? How are they currently missing in my life? What do I need to do to bring more of them into my life?" I knew those answers would be the hidden gems that would help me discover what I needed to change and what choices I needed to make instead.

Here's what I discovered:

- **FREEDOM**: Freedom is my cornerstone. It's what defines everything that I am. Like I said at the beginning, I never want to feel like I am trapped in a box. I crave the freedom to create, think, and explore in all facets of my life, but I found myself stuck. I had a thriving practice. I had a great inner circle of people, but what I didn't have was freedom. It was hard to leave my practice for vacations because I would have to rearrange my patients' treatment schedules. I didn't like the feeling of having my work confined to a location, and I wanted to make a bigger impact. That led to a series of choices to create a lifestyle with more freedom. I sold my practice. I built an online business. I paved the way to become an entrepreneur, so I could do the work I wanted, when I wanted, wherever I wanted, and because of that, I found my freedom.

- **JOY**: Throughout my life, I've had people ask me: "How do you stay so happy all the time?" I always found that question shocking for two reasons. One, I choose to be happy. Two, we all have the right to be happy. I believe life should be joyful. It doesn't mean it won't present difficulties or challenges, but we choose to be joyful regardless. For me, when I'm happy, I'm alive. I'm giddy. My laugh is loud, and I'm beaming ear to ear. What makes me happy are appreciating the simple joys, acting like a kid, wit and sarcasm, being in the outdoors, staying active and eating clean, traveling to new destinations, among other things. So, when I found myself in a place in my life where I wasn't happy, I realized it was because I wasn't choosing to be happy, despite my circumstances, plus several of the things that made me happy were missing. I didn't make them a priority in my schedule, because I got too caught up in my work, which, ironically, used to make me happy but at the time no longer did. I was out of balance and out of sorts, so I rearranged my schedule. I planned ahead and looked to how I could make the things that make me happy more of a part of my life, both in what I do, who I surround myself with, and how I spend my time.

- **PASSION**: If I feel lackluster in my life, I know something is missing. I'm a passionate creature. I love to soak up what I can out of every experience. I thrive in the company of ideas, creative thinkers, seeking out challenges, and being amidst people who emanate a zest for life. It's why I crave long conversations, experiencing new things, pushing my physical limits, and being a voracious reader. I like to stimulate my brain, body, and soul with things that enrich me, and make me feel wildly alive. When I get stuck in routine, I get restless. When I'm surrounded by someone negative, I get salty. It's why I seek out the opposite and create a life where everything is filled with a sense of passion, from my goals to my relationships to my adventures.

Only by reflecting on your qualities can you determine to what extent you are living into them, or if you're actually ignoring them. Let's revisit the three questions I posed to you a few pages ago:

- Does your lifestyle reflect your qualities?
- Do the people in your life support those qualities or diminish them?
- Are the choices you're making on a day-to-day basis supporting those qualities?

Write down each quality on a piece of paper. For each of these questions, if your answer is no, then write out why. What is missing in your lifestyle? What are the people in your life not bringing to you? What choices aren't serving you?

Then, think about what you need to do to make those qualities a priority in your life. What do you need to incorporate into your lifestyle? What types of people do you want to attract? What are new choices you can make that will empower you? What experiences can you create to bring those qualities to life?

It's this type of due diligence that helps you live a life according to the priorities that are the most important to you — and start doing it *now*.

A brief but important interlude about prioritizing experiences over things:

When I decided to become a digital nomad, one of my first steps was to sell or donate most everything I owned. Because my life would be 100 percent travel, I could only carry what I could fit in my SUV or my suitcase.

That was an eye-opening experience, because I realized how few of my things I actually used. Only a percentage of what I owned were things that I really enjoyed having and were a part of my life on a regular basis. I found myself using only a fraction of my clothes, my kitchen gadgets, my books, notes, etc.

What at first seemed overwhelming, even though I felt like I didn't have that much stuff, actually became liberating. All the things I was holding onto to use at a later date were just things. And the things that made me "happy" were very few.

So, minimizing my possessions to what could fit into an SUV became an exercise of liberation, because I could actually focus and prioritize what experiences I wanted to fill my life, not what things I needed to take care of. It made me fully realize that what brings us the most fulfillment in life is going to come down to experiences over things.

Whether we're looking at material things or mental "things" like excuses or doubts, we accumulate them as we grow and just drag them along as things to be maintained like a car, without giving ourselves the chance to reassess what things we've piled up along the way.

This part of your journey is about undergoing a cleansing, if you will, that's designed to be therapeutic, so you can rebuild your mind and your life with a clean slate. Doing so will ensure that you don't build a 90-day plan to assemble new things, but rather, to focus on accumulating a new sense of self and way of living.

If there should be any priority in life, it is to focus on the experiences that will give you joy.

When our life ends, our stuff doesn't come with us, and typically the things we feel we are missing out on really aren't "things" at all, but rather experiences.

Even if you desire to bring a material possession into your life, it's more about the experience that thing can give you, than it is about the thing itself.

- Maybe you want a sports car, because you love the feeling of adrenaline and want to make adventure more of a priority in your life.

- Maybe you want a new piece of clothing or jewelry, because you want to feel more beautiful and see the importance of prioritizing yourself and self-care more.

- Maybe you want to travel to a remote destination somewhere in the world, because you realize that freedom and exploration are important priorities for you.

You see, it's more about the experience that thing gives you than the thing itself. That being said, if there is a thing that you've been wanting to bring into your life, and it is something that can bring you pure joy and bliss, then that is something to listen to.

But remember: The end-result is the experience that thing delivers.

To get you prepared for Section 3, let's take this one layer deeper and build out your priority list for your 90-Day Life Challenge, so that you can start to achieve three things:

1. Experience more joy in your day-to-day life.

2. Live into the qualities that make you feel truly alive, and bring out your authentic self.

3. Build the foundation for the goals you are going to set for yourself in the next 90 days.

Our priorities in life typically fall into one of four categories, which we introduced in Chapter 2: Mapping Choices, so first, let's identify what each of these categories means to you.

If you were living into your best self, how would you be thriving in each of these areas of life? What experiences would you be having in your:

- Love & Relationships: _____
- Health & Well-being: _____
- Purpose & Abundance: _____
- Adventures & Exploration: _____

In your answers, notice what is missing. What experiences do you want to have but currently don't? You will soon see in Section 3 that these areas will shape the goals you will set out to achieve in the next 90 days.

It is important to note here that the experiences you want to create should be something that can give you a sense of transformation, not just instant gratification. Think about experiences that can bring you satisfaction today, but also momentum to create more of them in the long-term.

When you can fill your life with enriching experiences, that is the hallmark of making you, and the best version of you, the top priority in your life.

Section 3:

90-DAY LIFE PLAN

The journey that lies ahead of you is one of transformation, heightened purpose, and newfound joy in your life.

HOW YOU WILL TRANSFORM YOUR LIFE IN 90 DAYS

THIS SECTION IS about transformation. It's about having a clear direction for where you want to take your life, so that you can reawaken your sense of happiness and fulfillment in 90 days.

In the first two sections, we focused on tearing down the walls of what has been holding you back from living into your greatest self. We worked through the path of choices you've made and circumstances you currently experience, so you can predict your regrets ahead of time. We did this so that you could have the forethought to decide what you like about the direction of your life now and what you need to shift in your path. This opens up the space for new changes, for novel ideas, and for taking action. That is why we also addressed your biggest fears and areas of self-sabotage, so you can reconnect with that authentic version of you, the version where you feel the greatest joy. From this place, you were able to focus on your core priorities and the qualities with which you want to live your life.

Now we will build new layers of a new you. The way this section is designed is:

- First, I will show you the power of what 90 days can do for you, why we're using 90 days as the period for your life challenge, and how to embrace the impermanence that you are given in this timeframe.

- Next, I will walk you through the (4) 90-Day Life Areas. Using the awareness you gained from learning how to overcome your fears and build a new set of priorities, we will channel this into four sets of clear, precise goals that will elevate your way of life.

- Then, I will lay out your full 90-Day Life Challenge plan. This will be the structure for you to accomplish the goals and new life direction you are setting out to commit to. I will give you one challenge to focus on every 10 days, so by the time you have completed each of the nine challenges, you will have built a happier, more fulfilled you.

All the hard work that we have done together up to this point has paid off, because you now have a clearer understanding of who you are, what you want, and the life you are capable of creating.

Let's create your 90-Day Life Challenge...

CHAPTER 9:

WHY 90 DAYS

"Goals aren't enough. You need goals plus deadlines: goals big enough to get excited about and deadlines to make you run. One isn't much good without the other, but together they can be tremendous."

— BEN FELDMAN

I **UNDERSTAND THAT** this may seem a little ironic because on the surface it may appear that I am encouraging you to live as much of your life as possible in a 90-day period. I am doing this to encourage you to take action. You know that you can't take time for granted, but you know that you have.

You also know that you can change your life in a moment, or wait your entire lifetime for the right moment to happen.

What this 90-Day Life Challenge will do for you is create a short-enough period to spur you to choose action over procrastination, but long enough to create sustained results that will give you momentum after you complete it.

The goal here is transformation, yes, but it's not about crossing off every single item on your bucket list. This is about tapping back into who you really are and stop putting your dreams on hold. This is about remembering to tap into the power that you have to create a life you love, right now.

This is a journey that will be a transformation from your current life into a new version of yourself.

Part of this journey is letting go of the old thoughts, beliefs, and habits that have not been serving you, which is why we put so much focus on reflection and priorities before getting to this point.

There are a lot of different opinions[11] on how long it truly takes to form new habits. Earlier research has shown anywhere from 21 to 30 days, but the latest array of studies seems to have come to a new consensus.

In a study released in the European Journal of Social Psychology,[12] Phillippa Lally and her team of researchers surveyed 96 people over a 12-week period to find exactly how long it takes to form a new habit.

Over the 12 weeks, the participants chose a new habit and reported each day how automatic this new behavior felt. At the end of the period, Lally analyzed the results and found the average time it took for participants to pick up a new habit was 66 days.

These findings are invaluable, because they provide a clear timeline for what it takes to create new, sustained changes in your life.

Why Resolutions Never Work

According to U.S. News,[13] approximately 80 percent of resolutions fail by the second week of February. Despite a person's best efforts to change themselves, not even the turn of a new year creates enough motivation to stick with those changes.

Why are the odds against you?

In a world where instant gratification is the norm, we experience first-hand that changes can happen quickly, but the best changes actually occur over time. We can get almost any material thing we desire in a matter of a few days delivered to our doorstep. But to build a new life, it takes a commitment. It won't just happen in a two-day delivery.

It's why New Year's Resolutions don't work, because people give up on their goal and themselves too quickly. Those old habits and excuses like to take over, because they're the norm for us. It's what we know. New habits, however, take time to get ingrained and once they do, they become automatic and your new normal.

Like we discussed earlier in the book, our brains like habits because almost everything in our brain is built on the concept of a feedback loop. When our brain receives a stimulus, whether that's something in our environment like a sight or a smell or something within us like a thought, it will go through a feedback loop based on previous experiences to create a predictable reaction. Once our brain receives that stimulus, it will trigger the nerves in that feedback loop to create that reaction, like a behavior or emotion.

Feedback loops are the basis of everything. They are built from a collection of all our past experiences, and current experiences that reinforce those loops to make them stronger. For the feedback loops that don't serve you, like the self-sabotage loops, self-limiting definitions, and the like, the key to overcoming them is to create new habits based on the same stimuli, or change the stimuli altogether and do it over and over again until the new habit becomes a new automatic choice for your brain to assume.

Let's see how this plays out in a few examples...

> If one of your goals in your 90-Day Life Challenge is to lose weight, you'll want to create a new set of habits to achieve that goal. Maybe in the past you would see a donut and then eat that donut. But a new habit would be to see that donut, tell yourself, "I'm not interested," and walk away. Then every time you are tempted to eat junk food, you keep telling yourself, "I'm not interested." If you keep this up for 66 days, you will have built a new habit where you genuinely don't feel interested in that junk food, so it is no longer the craving that it once was.

> If one of your 90-day life priorities is to bring more abundance and wealth into your life, you'll want to build a new association around money. Perhaps in the past you would look at someone with more

prosperity than you and feel envious. That reaction is a habit. But a new habit would be to see that person and be grateful for the inspiration their success now gives to you.

See how one habit over time can transform your perception of yourself and your life? The power of incorporating these new habits over and over is that it will accumulate into a happier, more-fulfilled you, both in 90 days and for the long-term.

So why not do a 66-day challenge you ask?

It's one thing to make a new habit form, it's another to have a period to reinforce that habit and build in multiple habits over time. The 90-day period will allow you to have a very clear, set timeframe to achieve both.

In the chapters ahead, we are going to build a set of four types of goals that you will be able to schedule and structure over the course of nine different challenges. This will give you 10 days to focus on one core challenge at a time, then add on another new challenge every 10 days.

Not only will you be able to build in new habits, but you will be able to use this amount of time to act as your best accountability partner. I have seen the 90-day timeframe used successfully in a lot of business applications. I have also used it myself very successfully in approaching my own business goals, as well as applying it as a tool in my coaching and online programs. It's a common benchmark because it allows you to look at what you want to accomplish month by month, week by week, and day by day.

Typically, though, the application is in a business-centered environment, thinking of what you want to achieve in terms of leads, customers, revenue, and the like. So, I want to expand this concept into a different space, where you can apply it to your life as a whole and set goals in multiple areas of your life, not just one.

There is nothing better than having a goal set to a schedule. Without it, the goal can sit on a shelf getting dusty; with a schedule and deadline, you will be propelled to act.

Parkinson's Law

Parkinson's Law states the following: You will take as much time as you give to a task to complete it.

In other words, "Work expands to fill the time available for its completion."

Not one moment more or less. So, whether you choose to do something in 90 days or 90 years, you will take that long to finish it. You will take as long as you tell yourself you need to accomplish a task.

Remember back in school when you'd get an assignment and that assignment was due in a week? Were you the overachiever who started on the assignment right away and took the full week to get it done, or were you the procrastinator who stayed up all night the day before it was due to get it done?

Either way, you end up with the same result. You still end up getting the work done, whether you took seven days or seven hours to complete it. The pressure of time is what creates the fuel to get the task done.

Now think of how we apply the Parkinson's Law to our entire lives. We can take years to accomplish a dream because we keep putting it off, or we can focus on creating a path to achieve it in just a matter of weeks. This right here is what I mean about the art of embracing impermanence. Using the time that is right in front of you. Create shorter deadlines, so you don't procrastinate on your dreams.

Ultimately, it's your choice for how much time you want to give to the dream in front of you, and your 90-Day Life Challenge will allow you to use Parkinson's Law to your advantage.

Anthony Robbins has this great saying: "People overestimate what they can do in a day and underestimate what they can do in a decade." I love this approach to looking at success over the long term, but when it comes to using impermanence to fuel you, I like to think of it in the opposite way:

People overestimate what they can do in a lifetime and underestimate what they can do in a day.

Parkinson's Law helps you chase your dreams by establishing a timeline and renewed focus on what you want in your life. *Now.*

So, let's use it to your advantage to create a newfound motivation to make your goals happen quicker than what you once thought possible.

CHAPTER 10:

BEGIN WITH THE END IN MIND

"Life isn't about finding yourself.
Life is about creating yourself."

– GEORGE BERNARD SHAW

LET'S FAST-FORWARD TO the future for a moment. Imagine with me that it's Day 90. You have just finished your 90-Day Life Challenge, and you're about to start a new chapter in your life. You will wake up tomorrow and it's a new Day 1 for you.

Close your eyes for a moment. Tell me, what do you see? Who is the person you want to become? What is that version of you doing? What have you accomplished? Think about everything you have learned about yourself at this point. Think about all the different questions, statements, and exercises I have walked you through to build a new level of self-awareness and hunger for change. What is it that you are ready to release? What is it that you want to achieve by committing to this challenge?

When we get into the next chapter, I will walk you through the (4) 90-Day Life Areas, so you can establish your goals for your challenge. These goals will be your **absolutes**. Meaning that, without compromise, these are the things you absolutely want to accomplish in this 90-day period. No excuses. No exceptions. You know that by accomplishing these things, you will have elevated yourself to a new quality of life.

These goals will give you a scaffolding, so you know the journey that you will be on. They will give you the direction you need, so you know what you're aiming for.

To understand what these absolutes are for you, you must begin with the end-result in mind.

The reason why life can drag on without change is that it's easy to get lost in busywork and things that don't really catapult your momentum. If you don't have a goal, monotony can sink in. You end up settling and feeling stuck.

When you are seeking to make changes in life and using goals to help you get there, it can be both exciting and overwhelming. A goal is something out there, in the future, in a newer version of yourself.

The reason why people fail to achieve their goals is simple. The gap between who you are now and who you plan to become can feel too vast, the journey too long to arrive at the end-result you have in mind. Our brain is trying to figure out how to bridge that gap and all the steps in front of you can seem overwhelming when you think about the distance you must travel.

The 90-Day Life Challenge is what will bridge that gap for you with a clear, step-by-step plan.

While gazing into the future has its place for creating motivation, we actually want to look at your 90-Day Life Challenge not from Day 1, but from Day 90. You want to do this before you actually set your goals in the (4) 90-Day Life Areas.

When you start with the end-result in mind, you'll have a clear vision of what you want to achieve and who you want to become.

So, before you focus on your specific goals in the next chapter, let's think about you on Day 90:

- What have you **accomplished**?
- What fears have you **overcome**?
- What **breakthroughs** did you have?
- What's the **transformation** you want to create?
- Ultimately, who are you now, and how is this **different** from the person you were on Day 1?

When you start with the end-result painted out, you have a clear focal point that you are looking toward, so every action you take is intentional to help you get one step closer to it and every moment is well spent, rather than wasted. The vision you create from your answers to these questions will reflect the culmination of the tangible goals you are about to set.

So rather than looking at the gap ahead, you can plot out how you are going to get there, because you know the destination. This is what's referred to as "reverse engineering" to achieve your goals. You work backward, so you can move forward. You start with the end in mind, so you know where you are going.

Once you understand what Day 90 looks like for you, then you can look ahead and determine what are you going to do during each of the nine challenges to reach your goals. This will allow you to pare down everything you want to accomplish and know where your focus is on a daily basis.

This process will create a clear path for success and remove any overwhelm that you could experience if you solely look ahead. You will better understand what you are doing, when you are doing it, and know exactly why you are doing it.

The 90-Day Letter

My clients refer to this exercise as "compelling, eye-opening, and mind-blowing." They say it truly transformed the way they look at their lives and how they're spending it. It's a powerful tool in accountability, because you write a letter to yourself on what your life will look like at the end of these 90 days.

This exercise is simple, yet incredibly powerful, because you are actually creating a way to be accountable to yourself. Yes, I am guiding you through this process, but as a coach, it is purely my job to show you the way. It is for you to take the opportunity in front of you to create the clarity and vision behind what you are learning.

In this exercise, you write a letter to yourself about the journey you have been on for 90 days. In this letter will be the answers to the questions on the previous page: What have you accomplished? What fears have you overcome? What breakthroughs did you have? What's the transformation you want to create? Ultimately, who are you now, and how is that different from the person you were on Day 1?

This is an exercise in visualization and clarity, so it is imperative that you do these three things to create an effective letter:

1. Start with a blank canvas. The creative part of your brain will like this because you can allow for a steady stream of free thoughts to come to you, so make sure you use your 90-Day Life Workbook or a blank piece of paper for this exercise.

2. Be limitless. That inner child in you wants to reawaken. Imagine if anything was possible, what would you do? What could you accomplish? Let your imagination flow, and if that adult brain starts to chime in with a doubt, tell it to go quiet, so you can listen to the playful, inspired side of you.

3. Take a minimum of 15 minutes to write this letter. You will want to give yourself the time to be in a distraction-free space just to yourself. The longer you stay in this space, the more your mind can think clearly and reflect.

Once you write your letter, re-read the letter and see what stands out to you. I would encourage you to find the themes in your letter. What are the words that stand out to you? What are the goals that have come out of this exercise? What qualities or traits have you declared as being part of you on Day 90? Take a moment and circle the different words and phrases that stand out to you, because those are the hints behind the goals you will set in the next chapter.

As we work through the (4) 90-Day Life Areas next, keep this letter close to you as a reference point for setting your goals. It is also likely that you will want to expand on your letter as you discover new things that you want to accomplish, so you can then refine the letter after you set your goals as needed.

Chapter 11:

THE FOUR LIFE AREAS

*"Ask yourself what is really important
and then have the courage to build
your life around your answer."*

— Lee Jampolsky

To create structure behind your goals and help you categorize what you want to accomplish, I'm going to break down the four 90-Day Life Areas for you in this chapter. Once you understand what your goals are, then you'll be able to lay out the plan to accomplish them, which we'll cover in the 90-Day Life Challenge Plan in the following chapter.

The (4) 90-Day Life Areas are the cornerstones of your journey. By focusing on your goals in each of these areas, you are harnessing the ability to enrich the quality of your life across the board.

When you apply time and focus in these areas, you will create a fulfilling daily experience in how you show up and what you put out into the world. They also provide you with a sense of balance. Too often in life, I think we can find ourselves experiencing tunnel vision, where we are focused so intently on one area of our lives that we let other parts of it go on autopilot, or we just let ourselves go altogether and focus on things outside of us.

Until one day we wake up and realize: "I haven't talked to my friends for a while. It's been forever since I've gone to the gym. I've been working 60 hours a week for as long as I can remember. I dread going into work."

We're going to look at this from a 30,000-foot view. As you map out your goals, I want you to look at the scope of your entire life right now and think about what you can do to create progress in several areas of your life and do it in a way where you can provide focus to each.

Did you ever play with race cars as a kid and line up the cars together? Then once the race started, did you find yourself inching along each car to push it forward, so one car didn't get too far ahead? You wanted to make sure that every car had a spot in the race and had a chance to win. You gave each car the turbo-boost it needed when it was falling behind, so it could catch up to the others. You never let one car get lost in the back or get lapped.

I think the game of life should be played like those kinds of races. We want all the cars to have a chance. We want all the cars to win, and we want the race to last forever. Creating a fulfilling life where you are on a constant journey of growth should be just like those race cars. Each car is inching forward and each car is in the game. No car is left behind. They're all in the race together.

That's what makes the race fun.

So, each of the four 90-Day Life Areas has been carefully designed to accelerate every area of your life, so you will feel more fulfilled, vibrant, and on purpose.

To map out your goal, we're going to use an exercise known as mind-mapping. Let me first share why mind-mapping is essential for your 90-Day Life Challenge, then I'll go through the (4) 90-Day Life Areas, why each area is important, and give you the opportunity to define your goals in each area.

Why Mind-mapping

Mind-mapping is an exercise that allows you to get all your ideas on paper as a visual way to brainstorm your goals.

You're going to create a mind map for each of the four life areas, and the core concept of that life area will be in the center of the paper. You'll brainstorm on this mind map like a flow chart or spider web of ideas coming from the core concept. Then with each idea, more ideas will sprout.

So, it will look something like this...

I love mind-mapping because we spend so much time on our laptops, tablets, and smartphones that we're losing the art of actually writing and drawing. When it comes to something creative like this, typing out ideas feels more regimented to me and boring because you're making a list.

With mind-mapping, you can get creative and play. You can draw, use colors, make it vibrant and a reflection of you. It creates a really freeing and creative space.

When you write something with your hand, as opposed to typing it on a keyboard, it opens up another creative area of your brain, which means it allows you to think on a different scale, a bigger scale, one less cluttered with preconceived notions, old feedback loops and comforts. You don't get the chance to do this often, if ever, so it is *novel*, which invites discovery and invention. You'll find that more freshly baked ideas come to you.

Mind-mapping gives you permission to keep brainstorming on these ideas for however long as you want to. So, what you'll want to have at the ready is your 90-Day Life Workbook or a large piece of paper like a sketch pad. Then I would spend at least fifteen minutes on each area, so you can allow yourself to focus purely on brainstorming and creating, just like you did for your 90-Day Letter.

You'll be surprised at what comes out of you using a creative tool like this. It makes you realize what ideas you have been hiding and what you have really been wanting to do that you just keep putting off.

Mind-maps also help you put it all out there, and allow you to look at your goals every day to both motivate you and to keep you accountable during your 90-Day Life Challenge.

Have Dreams that Scare You

"The size of your dreams must always exceed your current capacity to achieve them. If your dreams do not scare you, they are not big enough."

— ELLEN JOHNSON SIRLEAF

This 90-Day Life Challenge is more than doing a few things that you've been putting on hold. This is about creating something epic in your life. This is about waking up three months from now realizing that you have created more in your life in the past 90 days than you could have ever imagined you were capable of.

On the other side of the self-sabotage loops, fears, and choices you've been stuck in are dreams, courage, tenacity, and a hunger to act. At least one of the dreams you create for your 90-Day Life Challenge should scare you and make you think: "Can I really do this? Am I really capable of this? Can I really achieve this?" It should challenge you to face doubt, confront fear, and question yourself.

That's the direction your mind needs to go in. That's the level you need to step up to, because this is where you will break past the current limits that you have set for yourself.

When I embarked on my first 90-Day Life Challenge, one of my big dreams was to apply for a TED talk. I've been wanting to get into the speaking circuit for the past few years, but I've been too nervous and unsure of myself.

I also knew that I wanted to expand my impact beyond the health and wellness industry and help people, no matter what stage of life they're in, to create their lives now rather than wait for them to happen. That was the driving force that I knew I had to keep in focus despite my fear. I had to picture myself on that stage. I had to challenge myself to think about the message I wanted to share and what was the impact I've been really wanting to make. I had to face the fear or end up facing the regret that I never tried.

After a lot of reflection, I realized that everything I am about comes back to the core of breaking away from what the conventional path has taught me about how to live and what's possible, and to not put my life on the back burner. I realized that everything I had done up to this goal was actually part of the beautiful design to help me accomplish it, so I came up with the topic, "Why You Should Shorten Your Life."

I wanted my topic and title to create a stir when reading it and feel bolder than anything I had done before, and I knew that this was it. I knew because it scared me to put it out there. I knew in doing so I was declaring that I wanted to share my view on life and the unique lens I bring to the table. I knew that this was the essence of my message. This was the cornerstone of everything I love and preach about impermanence and making the most out of the time you have in front of you.

I remember the afternoon on Day 32 of my 90-Day Life Challenge as clear as day. I was staring at the speaker application page on Ted.com. I could feel my heart pounding in my chest. My brow started to sweat even though it was a cool fall day. *I was so nervous I felt like I could vomit.*

I don't know how long I just looked at the blank space below this question:

What might the TED talk be about?

It felt like hours, but I kept glancing at the time on my computer, realizing only minutes had passed. I was completely terrified, realizing that this moment was the epitome of facing my insecurities. I knew that by doing this I was declaring, "*I am ready. I am willing to commit. I will no longer settle for saying no to this dream.*"

It was a strange feeling of absolute clarity about what I wanted — and absolute terror at the sheer thought of it.

It's one thing to dream about doing something. It's another to take action toward it.

I have pictured myself on the TED stage. I've thought about what it would look like and feel like to be there. But this was making it real. This was a first huge step in declaring what I want the next chapter of my life to become.

I've spent the past several years looking up to entrepreneurs who have inspired me and found myself wishing I could be like them. I knew that submitting my TED talk was going to be a huge first step to putting that intention out there, and there was no looking back. Once I hit "submit," I wasn't going to look back, only forward.

Then I realized something important: I was building up the fear more in my mind than I actually realized, because what I was actually fearing was a simple action of submitting an application. It was just putting words on a page. It was simply submitting an idea. Beneath the surface of that action was a fear of what I could actually become, and that was a fear that had paralyzed me up until now.

Could I really be like the entrepreneurs I've looked up to for all these years? Could I really be in the company of them and be seen as a peer?

I knew I had to submit this application because by doing so, I couldn't just keep telling myself that I wanted to be like them. I had to declare, *I AM one of them.*

What I realized in this simple act of clicking "submit," is this:

Beyond the fear is great joy. Beyond the uncertainty lies great clarity. Beyond the doubt lies great action.

All it takes is action. One small step can change the course of your entire life. Fear is your ally, not your enemy. Fear is the thing that will challenge you more than anything in your life. It will prompt you to ask this one question, "Will you face it?"

It's time to let yourself feel scared again. Not for yourself, not for what could go wrong, but for what you can become.

The Four Driving Forces for Your 90-Day Life Challenge

In Chapter 2, I asked you to rank yourself on a scale from 0-10, with 0 meaning "no satisfaction" to 10 meaning "completely satisfied," in these four areas of your life:

- #1 Your Health
- #2 Your Relationships
- #3 Your Contribution
- #4 Your Personal Growth

Revisit how you scored yourself in that chapter. What were your scores? Why did you give yourself the numbers you did? If you aren't a 10 in each area, what is missing? What do you need to do to become a 10?

If you want to achieve a new level of greatness in your 90-Day Life Challenge, you need to determine: "What is the goal I need to set in each of these areas to score higher on Day 90 than I am today?" This is where your transformation will happen.

As we work through each of the four areas, I will provide you with questions as prompts to help you determine the goals you want to achieve. These prompts will help you "fill in the clouds" of your mind-maps and build out your vision for the next 90 days.

90-Day Life Area #1: Health and Thrive

"Take care of your body. It's the only place you have to live in."

– JIM ROHN

To flourish in your life, you must be operating at your highest capacity. Your health should be treated as something exquisite, because it is the most important asset you have. You also have the capacity to improve and sustain your health throughout the course of your life, because getting old doesn't have to mean you just let yourself go.

We will start mapping out your goals in the area of health first, because it will be the cornerstone for you to operate in other areas of your life from a place of high energy, mental clarity, and physical endurance. This area is also naturally an area where people tend to crave the most improvement inherently. Most people aren't as healthy as they want to be, but they let the clutter of life get in the way of making it a priority. By starting with your health, you're going to put yourself first.

While most people base their health on the number on the scale, we're going to look at this from a different lens. I want you to think about your health with the perspective of using your health to thrive in life. I want you to embrace that if you can elevate your physical and mental capacity more in 90 days from where you currently stand today, you will be able to function at a higher level.

The one thing that is constant in your journey is your mind and your body. You always have that with you. It is the truest home that we all have. Everything that you hold onto — your thoughts, ideas, beliefs, injuries, doubts, strengths, fears, concerns, and joys — all reside within you.

So, to start to establish your 90-day goals in this area, ask yourself this: "How well are you taking care of your home?"

Because without health, we have nothing. And it is so, so easy to take our health for granted. It's during the times of injuries, ailments, and disease that we realize just how much we value our health, and we'd give anything to have it back.

This is an opportunity to evaluate your current level of health. Are you taking care of yourself the way you want to? Do you want to move to another level physically, energetically, mentally?

Your goals in this section should be designed to enhance your well-being on all of these levels. It's not just about having a good bill of health. This is about being able to wake up every day feeling energized, vital, and alive, so you can put attention toward everything that is important to you.

Your mind and your body are beautifully intertwined. They work together, yet they function as one, which is why we're going to look at establishing goals in two areas – your physical health and your mental health.

First, your physical health. Think about the current state your body is in. Are you carrying a few extra pounds? Do you wake up energized or sluggish, only to deal with afternoon crashes later in the day? Are you dealing with aches and pains, or can you move and use your body the way you want? Can you be active and do the things you enjoy?

To help you define your goals, it's helpful to hold up a mirror and really evaluate yourself. Knowing where your physical health is lacking is what will help you set goals to improve it.

Here are some prompts to help you determine what your physical health goals should be:

1. By Day 90, I want to be in this physical condition: _____. This is where you can use benchmark goals like weight, body fat percentage, size of clothes you wear, so you can attach a tangible number to your goal.

2. The physical activity I want to be able to do by Day 90 is: _____. Maybe you want to run a race, compete in a sport, or play basketball with your kids.

3. This is something I can't do with my body now that I want to be able to do by Day 90: _____ _____.

I personally love this last prompt because it tends to pull at a few heartstrings. I would encourage you to think of something you want to do but no longer can or something you have never done but always wanted to. Maybe you want to learn how to swim, but you've been too afraid of the water. Maybe you want to ski again but haven't because of previous injuries. Think about the physical activities you are missing out on.

Now that you understand your physical health goals, let's take time on focus on your mental health.

This is often a neglected area of our health, because it's not visual. It's easier to focus on the health of our body, because it's what we can see. It's tangible. You can notice the difference in your body by how you look, move, and feel as you work toward your goals. It's easier to chart your progress.

But your perception of yourself and your life is everything. Your mental health drives your level of joy and satisfaction in the world. It's the most important asset to your health that you have. You could be at your perfect weight, but if you have negative self-talk, it won't feel good enough. You may have achieved a goal of running a marathon, but you could limit your ability to celebrate your achievement because you didn't run as fast as you thought you should have.

The purpose here is to elevate how you view yourself in every moment and what you are doing to create a higher state of thoughts, feelings, and behaviors to build a positive outlook on yourself and your life.

Use the following statements to help you determine your 90-Day mental health goals:

- The emotion I want to feel on a daily basis is: ____
  _____. How will you act differently as a result of feeling this way?

- The perception I want to have of myself by Day 90 is:
  _____. Think about how you want to talk about yourself. If you were to describe yourself at your best to someone you love, what would you say?

- I want to focus on cultivating my learning and personal growth by committing to the following: ____
  _____. For this statement, think about activities that can nurture your mental health, such as affirmations, meditation, yoga, visualization exercises, and reading.

How good you feel about yourself mentally will directly influence how you feel about your body and vice versa. The more you cultivate your mental health, the more driven and inspired you will feel.

90-Day Life Area #2: Love and Give

Love. It's what makes the world go round. The more we put out into the world and within ourselves, the more fulfilling our life will be.

This section is all about setting goals that will improve the course of your relationships, starting with the relationship that you have with yourself and then going out from there.

At the end of your life, you will never question if you worked hard enough or spent too much time doing things that don't really matter. You will question things like: "Did I spend enough time with my family? Was I a good friend? Was I a supportive partner?"

This 90-Day Life Area is powerful, because it creates a catalyst to propel you to view the way you express love and experience love in a different way. It's a fundamental reminder to focus on the things that are important to you now, including yourself, rather than wishing you would've done more of them earlier in life.

I see "love and give" as a cycle, in that what you put out into the world will come back to you in return. We're going to look at different types of love and how that translates into how much you give. The idea here is to create goals that elevate your level of compassion and kindness, so you can look back on Day 90 knowing that you truly loved, in all ways.

LOVE OF YOURSELF

First, you want to think about how you can bring more self-love into your world. Remember when we redefined getting selfish? This is where we're going to loop that concept into your goals and help you prioritize yourself first, so you can focus on your core needs, create a higher level of internal satisfaction, in turn giving you the energy to put more out into the world.

Use the following statements to help you determine your 90-day goals to love yourself:

- I am going to eliminate the following things that distract me or take up unnecessary time and energy: _____. Think about the things you are saying "yes" to because you feel compelled to do them, even though they bring you minimal to no satisfaction.

- I will make time to focus on self-care every day by doing the following: _____. Think about what you can incorporate into your routine to give you time to honor and take care of yourself.

- I will commit to incorporating this hobby or activity into my life routine, because I know it will give me joy: _____. Think about one thing you can do that will instantly make you feel happy, expressive, and like your authentic self. Perhaps it's a creative hobby like music or dancing, or it's a physical activity like riding your bike or going for a run. You may notice here that this also creates an opportunity for overlap. While these four 90-Day Life Areas are individual and distinct, start to pay attention to how goals in one area can serve goals in another.

The more you can love from within, the more love you are able to give.

LOVE OF YOUR INNER CIRCLE

Next, naturally, is to create goals based on how you can bring more love to the people you're closest to, your family and your friends.

Sometimes it's easy to take your loved ones for granted because they're always there for you. They love you unconditionally, and they will do anything for you.

So, use these questions to think about goals to love and appreciate your inner circle more over the next 90 days:

- What can you do to make the people in your life feel deeply appreciated and loved by you?

- What haven't you done for them in a while that you used to?

- What can you do to express that you love someone unconditionally? Think about ways you can give to someone purely for the act and pleasure of giving, without expecting anything in return.

- Is there someone in your inner circle that you haven't spoken to or seen in a long time? Perhaps you have a long-lost friend who you haven't talked to for years, but you know if you did, you would pick right up where you left off.

When you care for your inner circle, you in turn will experience the joy of knowing that you've shown up and loved them as an amazing partner, son, daughter, sibling, and friend.

LOVE OF YOUR COMMUNITY

The definition of community is broader now than ever. It's easier for people to change locations frequently and build virtual relationships with a community of people from anywhere in the world. With modern communication, the world is at your fingertips. Community is no longer confined to the zip code you live in. It's a part of the picture, but not the whole picture.

Think about your definition of community. What does community mean to you? How would you describe the different communities you are a part of?

Because I'm an entrepreneur, my online community is a huge part of my purpose. How can I support the people who follow me and choose to work with me? How can I serve them and help them experience more fulfillment in their life? They are a huge part of my why. Because I travel frequently, I love the flexibility, while at the same time do what I can to truly immerse myself in the community I live in at the time. I like to be able to live like a local and truly feel like a part of their world, because for however long I live in one location, I am.

Our community, be that physical or online, is part of our natural surroundings. It's what we live and breathe every day. What we give to our community is part of what will shape the experience we have existing in it, so this is an opportunity to re-center on the communities you are in.

Use the following statements to create your goals around love of your community:

- I am going to make more time for my community by doing the following: _____.

- I am going to give back to the community by making time for this: _____.
As a personal example, I actively participate in local causes I care about, like preservation of natural lands and trail clean-ups. And because of that, I feel instantly more at home, and use this same approach no matter where I live to create that same feeling, anywhere in the world.

This can apply to your physical and/or online community. If you have both, you have even more opportunities to love and give to both.

LOVE OF THE WORLD

In love of the world, there is a plethora of opportunity for loving and giving, as there are so many different ways we can all individually contribute to the world we live in. For some, it may mean focusing on environmental causes. For others, it may mean purely leading by example by treating people with kindness and compassion, no matter who they are. And in today's time, there's more opportunity to make a global impact by doing things like creating online businesses and contributing to charities, so you can share your message, your knowledge, and your compassion with people all over the world.

The opportunities here are endless and life-enriching. It is not my responsibility to help define this for you, but rather to give you the fire-starter questions to get you thinking about what setting goals here means for you:

- What is a gift, strength, or resource that you have that can be used to create a domino effect of goodwill or kindness?

- How do you want to give back to the world?

- Is there a cause you care about that you would like to get involved in? I care about using my own prosperity to give back to causes I care about, which is why I donate a portion of my business profits to **Kiva.org**, a nonprofit organization that offers micro-loans to startup businesses for people all over the world. I commit to contributing to Kiva every month to help fellow entrepreneurs launch their own businesses and dreams. It's an opportunity for me to give back more as a result of my abundance.

As you can see, we are taking the concept of "love and give" and expanding out further and further. We are broadening our own definition of how we bring love to ourselves and to the world, focusing on us as the center, so that our love can grow outwards from there.

In the end, love is what really matters. How much you love and give of yourself will be the driving force to leading a fulfilling life. It is also the perspective you will bring into the next 90-Day Life Area.

90-Day Life Area #3: Serve and Succeed

Note that I'm putting this life area third, not first. While these four life areas aren't ranked in a sense, they are ordered in a way to build a core foundation, so you can grow from one area to the next.

This mind-map is all about two things: contribution and impact. We spend the majority of our waking hours focusing on our work, so it's vital to make sure the work we are doing is creating a sense of deep purpose within us. You should be excited to wake up every morning and get to do the things you do.

Being able to achieve this comes down to these two things:

1. Your ability to focus on "why" you do what you do, not just get lost in the "what" you must do to get the work done. The why is where your purpose lies, and the reason why I believe more people are unfulfilled with their work now more than ever

before is because they are too focused on the what, rather than their why.

2. Your free will to leverage your strengths. Your life's work, whether that's your career or your business or a combination of the two, should be the vehicle for you to be able to utilize your best strengths. You have the choice to do work that makes you feel like you are truly making a difference.

I think as a society we can get lost in the goals, the successes, and what we want to achieve individually. That's why I combine the concept of "serve" with "succeed," because I believe that the more you focus on your purpose and contribution, the more you're going to be able to succeed. It's the desire to serve that drives your success, not the other way around.

Use the following prompts to define your goals in this area:

- I will wake up every morning excited to start my day by focusing on doing work that cultivates this purpose: _____.

- My #1 strength that will help me live into my purpose is this: _____.

- The way I intend to utilize my strength more over the next 90 days is by doing the following: _____ _____.

- If I commit to doing this one thing in the next 90 days, I will be able to achieve this pinnacle of success in my life: _____.

In this last statement, I want you to think of something groundbreaking. Imagine you were designing your own "Lifetime Achievement Award" that you are destined to receive by accomplishing this one thing. Odds are that this dream may scare you. It may take some decisive action to make it happen. Remember, your dreams should be big enough to scare you. The more fear you feel, the higher the priority this goal should have.

90-Day Life Area #4: Adventures and Fears

Burnout in life can happen when our lives become all work and no play. Where's the fun in that?

Part of what makes life beautiful is that there is a playground of adventures and experiences waiting for each and every one of us. The only thing that is standing in your way to make them happen in your own life is fear, so you need to overcome your fears to make these experiences a priority.

I like to think of this 90-Day Life Area as where the classic bucket list goals lie. I encourage you to have fun in this section. Let your mind wander and play as you ponder all the fun that you want to have in this beautiful ride called life. Think about the crazy, wild ideas and adventures that you've been wanting to do for some time, but you've been putting off because you're telling yourself that:

...you're too afraid.

...you're too young.

...you're too old.

...you have to wait until you retire.

...you don't know how.

...you're too scared to try.

I tie together adventure with fear because I believe past every fear lies a great adventure. It doesn't mean you won't feel the fear. It simply means you won't let it hold you back.

The whole idea here is to think about the things that completely scare you, because on the opposite side of that fear, lies an awesome sense of accomplishment from doing it now at this stage of your life, rather than putting it on hold.

If you wait until a later point in your life, perhaps you won't be able to cross these things off your bucket list.

Remember the art of embracing impermanence. Take advantage of the 90 days in front of you and embrace the adventures you've always wanted to do.

So, this is really going to push you to break through the fears that hold you back, so you can play more in your life and just go for it. What's really important is to ask yourself: "What does adventure mean to me?" For some, adventure could mean doing something crazy in the great outdoors. For others, adventure could mean taking the leap to start your own business or ask someone you like out for a date.

Life can be full of adventures if we just look around and see what we've been holding out on. *The bigger the fear, the more exciting the adventure on the other side, and the bigger the reward.*

To create your 90-day adventure goals, contemplate the following statements:

- The fear that has been holding me back that I commit to overcoming in the next 90 days is: _____ _____.

- The adventure I will plan during the next 90 days —the one that lies on the other side of this fear — is: _____.

- The sense of accomplishment I will feel by experiencing this adventure is: _____ _____.

So, when it comes to adventures and fears, the domino effect you can experience is pure joy and a renewed sense of vigor in your life.

Mind Mapping the Four 90-Day Life Areas

Now that we have worked through these four areas, I want you to place the answers to your statements onto mind-maps, so you have a visual chart of your goals that you want to commit to doing in the next 90 days.

Use your 90-Day Life Workbook or sketch page and create four mind-maps, each on a separate piece of paper.

Label each of the pages with the life area in the middle:

- #1 Health and Thrive
- #2 Love and Give
- #3 Serve and Succeed
- #4 Adventures and Fears

Then work out from that area and start to identify core goals and themes that you want to focus on in your 90-Day Life Challenge. Use the answers from your statements and questions in each of the four sections and write them down on the appropriate mind map.

Note that as you do this, you will come up with a number of different goals and ideas for what to focus on. This is designed as a brainstorming exercise; this is not and should not be an exhaustive list. It's to help you get down all of the goals that come to mind on paper, so you can look at what you want to achieve in the next 90 days from a larger scale, and then look at what goals are most important to you to complete during that timeframe. By starting with the big picture and looking at everything on one page, you can start to hone in on what goals stand out most to you, so we can scale this into an inspiring as well as realistic personal transformation.

When you complete each mind map, step away from it so you can look at the entire thing. Review all the goals that you put on paper and ask yourself: "If I had to rank my goals, in order of importance of which are the most important to me, how would I rank them?"

Place numbers next to each of those goals, so you can determine which ones are the most important to you, because those are the goals that you will focus on for your 90-Day Life Challenge.

Then, in each of the (4) 90-Day Life Areas, I would put a star next to the top three goals, so that you have a total of 12 goals to consider for your 90-Day Life Challenge.

I understand that 12 goals may seem like an extensive list to have and ask of yourself in 90 days. I am not going to set the expectation that you will accomplish all 12 of those goals, because what you want to achieve will determine the amount of planning, time, and effort it will take to accomplish each goal. What I am setting the expectation for in doing this exercise is to equip you with a broader life perspective, so you can see what it is that you want most to accomplish in your near future, as well as set the momentum for goals you want to achieve beyond 90 days.

You may find that it's best to pick three of those goals and solely focus on them, or you may decide to focus on all 12 and set the bar high to crush it. It is up to you how intense you want the pace to be and how high of a standard you want to expect. What I am doing is giving you the freedom within a framework. You have up to 12 goals to focus on in 90 days. I would at minimum focus on 3, and then build from there.

As we go into the next chapter and build your 90-Day Life Challenge plan, I will help you determine how to schedule your goals into this timeframe, so you have both realistic expectations of what you want to achieve and can set a motivating, maybe even slightly aggressive, schedule to achieve them. This will allow you to actually see how much you are capable of achieving in a short amount of time. The goal here is to push yourself, not create overwhelm. There is a fine balance between the two, which is why we'll create core challenges for you to focus on and place your goals within. That way you can stay focused on what's important to you and build momentum with each progressive challenge.

CHAPTER 12:

YOUR 90-DAY LIFE CHALLENGE PLAN

*"Ask yourself what is really important
and then have the courage to build
your life around your answer."*

— LEE JAMPOLSKY

ALL ROADS POINT to here. The work we have done together in the preceding chapters is what has prepared you for this stage, so you can take action and begin your 90-Day Life Challenge.

The journey ahead of you will be liberating, transformative, and life-changing. I won't pretend it will be an easy journey, because that is not the point. The point is that you are about to embark on a journey that will set your goals into action, push your limits, challenge the way you have viewed yourself, and reveal a new way of life and purpose.

In this chapter, I'm going to give you the road map to follow, so you know how to have a successful 90-Day Life Challenge. In this map, you will have a structure, so you understand what you are doing and what you will be focusing on every day for the next 90 days.

Your 90-Day Life Challenge road map is designed as a course that covers nine stages.

Every 10 days for the next 90 days, you are going to be given a challenge. This challenge will push you to channel your goals into action. As you will soon see, each challenge has a theme derived from a previous lesson you've learned in this book. We will start with fundamental themes, so you can build a solid foundation to work from, and then more specific themes and challenges as you progress.

These challenges are designed to be built off of one another. One naturally leads into the next to create more growth and momentum based on your work in the previous challenge. Just like the work you have done up to this point will prepare you to start, each successive challenge will prepare you for the next challenge ahead.

While you can certainly customize your approach to your 90-Day Life Challenge, I would highly recommend that you follow these challenges in the order given. My clients have experienced the best results when they focus linearly on each challenge. They have a clear sense of direction rather than feeling overwhelmed. They are able to accomplish their goals, create faster growth, and experience more transformations by using the structure I'm about to share with you.

**My promise to you is simple, but
my goal for you is grand.**

I intend to give you a road map that will rebuild your way of life in 90 days. I'm going to show you what you can achieve in a short amount of time. I am going to help you feel more on fire, more on purpose, and more in love with life than you ever have been before. It is my hope and plan that you will wake up on Day 90 proud of who you have become and what you have accomplished, so you have momentum going into this next chapter of your life.

You know the end-result you want to achieve. You know the goals you want to accomplish. You also know what accomplishing these goals will mean to you.

Before you actually start your 90-Day Life Challenge, I would highly recommend that you read this entire section first, so you can understand the full road map and progression of challenges that I have laid out for your journey, as well as where to place your goals.

So, let's get you started on your path and begin with Challenge #1.

Days 1-10: Set Your Schedule and Habits

*"Ask yourself if what you're doing
today is getting you closer to where
you want to be tomorrow."*

— UNKNOWN

At the start of any new venture, there is naturally going to be a lot of excitement and hope. This will be the emotional fuel to give you a great kick-start to your 90-Day Life Challenge.

To support your kick-start, you need to create a structure for this challenge on a day-by-day, week-by-week, and month-by-month basis.

Excitement and positivity will take you far, but it takes more than waking up with a new vigor to start each day. You must have a game plan in front of you to take action on the goals that you laid out in your (4) 90-Day Life Mind-maps, which is why your first challenge is going to focus on building out your structure for the next 90 days and then focusing on the core set of steps and habits to plot out, so you can make systematic progress toward each goal.

Step #1: Your first step in this challenge is to go back and **revisit the end-result** you want to achieve in this 90-Day Life Challenge. Go back to your answers to these questions: By Day 90, what have you accomplished? What fears have you overcome? What breakthroughs did you have? What's the transformation you want to create? Ultimately, who are you now, and how is that different from the person you were on Day 1?

This end-result is the driving force behind your focus for the next 90 days. Every thought, belief, goal, decision, and action should support this.

**Remember: to move forward,
you have to look backwards.
Begin with the end in mind.**

Step #2: Go grab your calendar. Your calendar is going to be one of your best assets for the next 90 days. It doesn't matter if it's a weekly planner, desktop calendar, or a calendar on one of your devices. Just make sure that it's a calendar you use as a part of your regular routine. I need you to be accustomed to looking at it, so you can start every day reminding yourself of the current challenge you are in and the current steps you are taking to reach your goals.

Now look at your calendar and decide on one date: The start date for your 90-Day Life Challenge. Mark that date on your calendar now. Make it obvious. Put circles around it. Draw arrows. Add smiley face stickers (big fan of this). Do what you need to make it stand out.

Then number each day, starting with Day 1, until you get to Day 90 and then repeat the same process for your final day that you did for Day 1. Make it loud and vibrant, so you simply cannot miss it in your calendar.

Once you declare these dates on the calendar, your 90-Day Life Challenge will transform to something you've been thinking about doing to something you ARE doing. Now you know the 90-day period that lies in front of you.

Making the commitment to dates not only in your mind now, but by actually putting them in your calendar will propel you to start your 90-Day Life Challenge and get rolling.

Without the structure, procrastination can kick in, and it gets easier to tell yourself, "I'll get to that tomorrow. Or maybe I'll wait until Monday."

Time is of the essence here. Remember, this is about taking action now. NOT putting your dreams on hold.

Step #3: Get Your 90-Day Letter. Or write it out if you haven't done it yet. You will want to print it out, sign it, and seal it in an envelope. Then on the envelope, write on the outside "do not open until (insert date), which will be Day 90. Sealing it with the date creates the intention for the schedule you have set.

I should mention that this letter is solely for you. I would encourage you to make this something private that only you reflect on and only you read on Day 90. Doing so creates an opportunity to reflect solely on your journey at this time and to do it intentionally. You need that space to be with yourself to take in the reflections of that moment when you read through it. It's very powerful when you can read something that you wrote solely for you.

Step #4: Schedule Your Goals. Go to your mind maps and look at the different goals you set in the (4) 90-Day Life Areas: (1) Health & Thrive, (2) Love & Give, (3) Serve and Succeed, (4) Adventures & Fears.

Now we are going to take those goals and create deadlines for each of them, so you can plot out dates during your

90-day period for when you intend to accomplish each goal.

There are a few ways to approach scheduling your goals.

First, it's really helpful to categorize the goals based on time. *How much time will it take to accomplish a goal?*

Is this a long-term goal that you will need to work toward and spend time on? Examples may be launching a new business venture or reaching a health goal. Or is this a short-term goal that just musters a dose of courage to get it done, like going skydiving or bungee jumping?

Two different types of goals requiring two different levels of commitment and focus. Both provide the same satisfaction of accomplishment.

Once you understand your short-term goals versus long-term goals, you can start to determine achievement dates for each of those goals during your 90-Day Life Challenge.

Use this statement as a framework to create a set of deadlines to achieve your goals in each of the four areas within 90 days:

> By this (insert date), I commit to accomplishing (this goal).

This will give you the framework to look ahead at each of those dates and then determine what you need to do (tangible actions or milestones) to accomplish each of those goals, so you can schedule them in your 90-day period.

Step #5: Identify Three Steps Per Goal: With your schedule in place, now you want to create a structure to work backward from the dates for each goal and determine what you need to do, by what time, to make them happen.

That's why I encourage you to focus on identifying three steps that you need to take with each goal. If you have these steps laid out in front of you, you can better determine what you need to do every day and week to accomplish those intermediate steps and make continual progress toward your goals.

So, with each of your 90-Day Goals, ask yourself this: "What are the three steps I absolutely must take over the next 90 days in order to achieve this goal?" Each step may be a singular task, or it may be a daily habit. For example, if one of your goals is to lose 10 pounds, then a singular task may be signing up for a gym membership, whereas a daily habit may be exercising for 60 minutes a day.

Understanding the difference will help you schedule out these steps, working backwards from the deadlines you have set, so you can determine what you are focusing on every day to achieve them.

Step #6: Eliminate Clutter: In order to have a successful 90-Day Life Challenge, you need clarity. To create clarity, you need to get rid of the clutter that's getting in your way, whether that's physical clutter or mental clutter.

Clutter is nothing but things we hold onto, so we can stay safe and be comforted by what we know. But clutter is really just a mess of the things that are holding you back or weighing you down.

To make room for your goals and the steps you've laid out to achieve them, you need to eliminate the things in your day-to-day life that are taking up your precious time, thoughts, and resources and aren't serving you. Those could be material things sitting around your house that you haven't used in ages but are holding onto. They could be self-limiting thoughts that are feeding your mind with doubt and insecurity. They could be distractions that do nothing but pull your focus away from yourself, like:

...flipping the channels or binge-watching TV shows.

...mindlessly scrolling through social media and email.

If you can cleanse the clutter from your life, you won't be distracted by the things that don't matter and will focus on the things that do.

Step #7: Establish New Habits. The clutter in your life is an accumulation of old habits and attachments. Once you remove this from your life, you can establish new habits that will support the goals you have and the steps you have laid out to achieve them.

For each of the goals you have declared for your 90-Day Life Challenge, I want you to consider what is one new habit you can incorporate into your daily life that will support those goals. These habits should be easy to implement right out of the gate. Think of a small habit you can start with per goal, so you can give each goal the attention it deserves and try not to take on a lot of massive change at once. For example, a small habit can be committing five minutes in the morning to visualizing your goals.

Once you have identified your habits, then go back to your calendar and schedule a time every day that you can focus on incorporating this habit into your life. Think of this as making appointments for yourself. You are carving out time to commit to what's important to you and stick with it.

These seven steps are instrumental in creating a solid foundation you can build upon for the next stage of your 90-Day Life Challenge.

Challenge #1 is really all about rebuilding you by shifting your focus to what you want to achieve, making deadlines for achieving those goals, and creating a set of core steps and habits to foster continued growth. The schedule you have created in these first 10 days will be the framework to ensure you are maximizing your time in every day of the challenge.

Days 11-20: Create Novelty

Now that you have established your core deadlines and set new habits, you are ready to embrace your next challenge.

For the next 10 days, we are going to focus on cultivating novelty in your life. This stems back to what we discussed in Chapter 5, and we're going to revisit the "routine flushing" exercise I introduced you to.

Novelty is the spice of life. If you recall, novelty has been shown to create not only instant gratification, but a feeling of sustained euphoria in your life. We inherently crave novelty but that desire often gets clouded by daily routine and monotony.

So, in this challenge, you're going to focus on creating novelty in your life every day for the next 10 days.

For day 1, your task is simple. I want you to go back to the routine flushing exercise and map out your daily routine:

> *Think about all the things you do consistently on a day-to-day basis. This should be very detailed, down to the simple tasks from when you take a shower to when you eat lunch. Think about what time of the day you do these things and how you do them, as well as the time of day you do them.*

Once you have mapped out your routine fully, I want you to step back and look at it. In the things that you do every single day, I want you to circle 10 of them. Pick 10 of the things that are the most automatic, boring, and monotonous. Think tasks like brushing your teeth or making the bed.

Then I want you to create a novel challenge for each task, one task a day for the next 10 days. Ask yourself: "How can I make this task feel fresh, new, and fun?" I want you to get creative with this. We are going to focus here on taking the mundane and making it fun.

We were so good about finding the joy in everything in life as children. Everything seemed like a game or an opportunity to play. Nothing was seen as serious, boring, or blah. This challenge will help you take the blahs out of your day and start to play again.

Here's another way to think about it: For each of the 10 tasks that you will turn into novel challenges, ask yourself, "How would the 5-year-old version of me do this?"

Here are some idea generators:

- Rather than sit home on a weeknight and watch TV, go out to the movies instead. Don't even pick a movie in advance. Just go and pick one when you get there.

- Don't take the same way home from work. See if you can drive through a new neighborhood or take the back roads and avoid the main highway.

- Instead of just brushing your teeth, dance around in your underwear while you do it. Yes, I'm being totally serious. Actually, I'm being totally goofy. We act too seriously as adults. Everything becomes a chore or a task, rather than an outlet for play.

That's the whole point of this challenge for days 11-20. I want to show you how simply you can change your state of being just by not taking yourself so seriously. I want you to see the power that even in your routines, there can be fun and novelty.

Life was meant to be fun, both in the simple things as well as the big adventures. Bring out that child that has been hiding in you.

The purpose of having this challenge here is to create momentum. Small changes in day-to-day tasks lead to big wins by creating more novelty in your life. Novelty is the needle-mover that can give you instant gratification. We want to stoke that fire, so you can feel a dose of euphoria every day in embracing something new. This will also set the stage for what's next, because, if you can build your muscles in novelty, you will be more open to bigger changes and taking bigger risks where the rewards will be that much sweeter.

Days 21-30: Take Courageous Action

The culprit that will rob you of your momentum in any point of your life, but particularly in your 90-Day Life Challenge, is fear, which is why we're going to face your fears early on in this journey.

This stage should feel scary because, for the next 10 days, I'm going to challenge you to take courageous action. Every day you are going to commit to doing something that will push you, something that will take your life and your limits to a new level. By the end of this challenge, you will have accomplished things you've been telling yourself that you've wanted to try for a long time, but you've been too scared to tackle.

Now is the time to face your fears. In this 10-day period, I will encourage you to pay special attention to the goals you set in Life Area #3: Serve & Succeed. Note that I am not having you focus on Life Area #4: Adventures & Fears, which is what you might expect. More on that to come in the next challenge. Hint, hint.

I want you to look at the goals you set for yourself in Life Area #3. Go back to your answer to this statement: If I commit to doing this one thing in the next 90 days, I will be able to achieve this pinnacle of success in my life:

_____.

What is that pinnacle of success for you? Why is that important to you and your purpose?

You know that the very thing that has been holding you back from reaching this success has been fear. Fear of the unknown, fear of failure, fear of success. Whatever that fear is, you also know that you put down your goal for a reason:

> There is courage underneath the fear, and the way you will find it is by pushing yourself to a new level.

The fear is actually there to help you find your courage, so now you're going to seek it out.

This challenge is designed to help you renew your purpose and elevate it, so I want you to think of that pinnacle of success and ask yourself:

> What is one bold, courageous action that I can take every day, for the next 10 days, to create massive momentum towards achieving that goal?

Imagine this, if you only had 10 days left on this earth, what would you do to accelerate making that goal happen as fast as possible. There is no room for busywork here. I'm talking about what are the steps you can take that will create the most movement and growth as possible.

- Maybe you want to connect with someone who has influence, but you've been too afraid to make the call.

- Maybe there is a conversation you've been wanting to have with your boss about a promotion, but you've been putting it off.

- Maybe you've been wanting to launch a new product in your business, but you've been unsure if the market will want it. What can you do to launch that product as fast as possible?

The steps you map out for the next 10 days should make your stomach churn a little, just like applying for my TED talk did. I will forewarn you, in fairness, that the first day will feel the hardest, because being courageous is a new act for most people.

Once you get a taste of courage on that first day, you will see that the greatest feeling comes not so much from the end-result of the step you have taken, but the fact that you took the courageous action in the first place. The courage in and of itself will be fulfilling. The momentum you achieve as a result will be like icing on the cake.

By focusing on courage for 10 days, you will also grow accustomed to the practice of it. It is my goal for you that you will find yourself saying: "That wasn't as scary as I thought," as you go into each successive day. The fear will still be there, but your ability to be courageous will be easier. Being able to use courage again and again for 10 days will start to make courage a habit. Again, that doesn't mean you won't be afraid, but you will use the fear to drive the change.

By the end of this challenge, not only will you feel more courageous, but you will have made huge leaps toward living more into your purpose and desire to succeed in this 90-day period.

Days 31-40: Seek Out Adventure

Now, my courageous friend, is when we'll start to step out of your comfort zone even further. You've already had 10 days to practice courage, how about 10 more, but in a different way?

In the last challenge, we focused on using courage to stimulate success in your life, by taking massive steps despite the fears you face.

Your courage muscles are stronger now. You're ready to channel that courage into adventure. Think of this 10-day challenge as your time to knock a thing or two off your bucket list.

I want you to go back to your 4th mind-map, and reflect back on these statements:

- The fear that has been holding me back that I commit to overcoming in the next 90 days is: _____
_____.

- The adventure I will plan during the next 90 days, the one that lies on the other side of this fear, is: ____
_____.

- The sense of accomplishment I will feel by experiencing this adventure is: _____
_____.

Focus on the adventure you have committed to. What do you need to do to complete that adventure in the next 10 days?

- Perhaps you take a last-minute flight to a dream destination.
- Or you call the local parasailing club and schedule a lesson.
- Or you finally sing at an open microphone night.

Typically, the adventure here is an event or an outing. Something that you can do once and feel complete about it. It doesn't mean that you won't do it again, but it's something that has been on your list that you have been putting off.

In this 10-day challenge, your time for putting that off stops now. You can actually cross that item off of your list.

Again, you will face fear in doing this. I encourage you to revisit the sense of accomplishment you will feel by achieving this often, and leading up to the date you've scheduled for your next adventure, this will support you by reminding you of why you want to do this in the first place.

There are two steps I would encourage you to take during this 10-day challenge that will help ensure you complete this adventure.

1. **Get an accountability partner.** You have built up the courage to do this adventure flying solo, but it's incredibly helpful if you can have an advocate by your side who is rooting you on to actually do

it. So, think of someone you can trust. It can be your partner, a parent, a sibling, a close friend. It should be someone you know who will hold you to what you say you want to do, not someone who will be nice and let you slide. You need a staunch supporter. Someone who will make sure you don't say no to yourself.

Once you pick this person, call them and tell them about the adventure you are committing to and the date you are committing to doing it. Then communicate what they can do to keep you accountable. You might want them to send you a text or call you that morning. Maybe you want them to reach out every day to provide a dose of motivation. Think about what would best serve you and make sure that this is something your accountability partner is not only willing to do, but excited to do.

Having this person in your corner will help you make this adventure happen and ensure that you are accountable to the most important thing, and that is you.

2. **Plan out your celebration.** Accomplishing something you have been putting on hold is one thing, but celebrating it is another. Before you take on your adventure, think about what you are going to do to celebrate it. Consider if you want to celebrate it by yourself or with others? What type of celebration would truly acknowledge what you just accomplished?

By planning out how you are going to celebrate your adventure, you are creating another layer of accountability for yourself, especially if you share your plans with others, and you will also create something to look forward to.

Because, after all, this entire process is something that is meant to be celebrated. Experiencing an adventure is something to be acknowledged. Remember that a huge part of this challenge is to help you find not only the end-result of who you want to become, but embrace the joy you are creating all along the way.

Days 41-50: Erase Resentment

For the past two challenges, we have really focused on creating quick momentum towards achieving your goals by using courage as your ally.

Courage manifests in all sorts of ways. From what you have experienced, it gives you the opportunity to face your fears and take action on the things you've been putting on hold.

This entire 90-Day journey is really a journey of courage, which is why now, I want you to reflect back on your life in this next challenge, for courage can help you not only face the fearful things, it can help you face difficult times.

That's why in this next 10-day period, it's important to pause and evaluate where in your life you hold any resentment. Throughout the course of our lives, we have been wronged in different ways. Things didn't fall into place. We've all been told no. People have mistreated you in some way.

It's imperative that you don't carry these wrongs with you in life, for all that will do is make you feel like a victim and look back at those times in your life with resentment, because resentment is the root of regret. The key to overcoming resentment or avoiding it altogether is looking back on your life up to this point as a culmination of experiences that have created you as you are today, and who you are right now is beautiful, strong, capable, confident, passionate, and vibrant. Even if you don't fully embrace all of that now, that is who you are becoming.

Transforming your quality of life doesn't just come in looking forward, it comes in looking back, so I want you to ask yourself the following questions:

- Who do you need to forgive?
- Why do you need to forgive them?
- What lessons have you learned from these people and periods of your life?
- Most importantly, what do you need to forgive in yourself?

I find this challenge to be quite profound in your 90-Day journey. These questions may bring up emotions that you have buried for some time. If you feel old memories or negative emotions resurfacing during this stage, be gentle with yourself and know that it's ok. You need to channel these emotions out of you, so you can live in a higher state of joy. I promise you that on the flip side of your answers to these questions, you will find peace in the forgiveness, because forgiveness is what will allow you to let go of your resentment.

As you can see, this is a very self-reflective phase of your journey. I would encourage you to take the first five days of this challenge and focus 100 percent on journaling your answers to these questions. Take time in your writing. Really think about the entire course of your life and the negative emotions you have built up within you during periods of strife or challenge.

Once you have clarity on this, then I would take the next five days to release this resentment. You can do this in one of two ways. I would actually recommend both, because it will create the most powerful change and shift towards forgiveness.

First, I would write a letter to yourself. This letter is all about how you forgive yourself for any of the wrongs you have done or felt guilty about. Once you write your letter, you need to release it, so either crumple it up in the trash or burn it, and let it go.

Then, I would look at the people you have resented in your life, and write a letter to them. In this letter, focus on the lessons you have learned from having them in your life. This is not an easy practice, but it is a powerful one that teaches you how to take the negative of anything and turn it into a positive. Share these lessons with the individual in your letter. Thank them for these lessons, for they are a part of what has shaped you to who you are today. Take power in that. See what good has come as a result.

At the end of our lives, if we're lucky and get the opportunity, we will think about the people who are in and have been in our lives. I think we all hope that we can reflect on everyone who has been in our journey from a place of peace, but often we can also have buried feelings of regret and resentment. These letters will help you release it. Now you can either choose to actually send these letters to the individuals, which I personally recommend, or you can let them go in the same way you did for your own. Trust which approach is going to give you the most peace and sense of completion.

This exercise was one of the most powerful experiences for me in my 90-Day Life Challenge. The hardest letter for me to write was a letter to my former boss, for whom I worked for two years. I used to hold a great deal of resentment toward him for the way he treated me as an employee. I felt bitter and dis-empowered. I felt like I wasted time in my life there. But as I went through this exercise myself, I realized something powerful. Because of him, I was able to discover more of what I wanted and not settle for a toxic job. Those two years actually set the stage for me to build my own practice, work with hundreds of patients, then become an entrepreneur and now impact thousands with my message. I realized that he was actually a blessing, for I learned things about myself that I may not have discovered otherwise or taken much longer to find.

Now I can say that I am genuinely grateful for him and what he brought to my life. I feel very much at peace and have become more loving of a person as a result.

This is the power of releasing resentment. You can let go of the weight of emotions that are holding you back, because the only person that resentment truly affects is you. In these 10 days, you have the power to take the emotional load off of you and no longer feel like a victim during periods of your life. Instead, you can look back on these periods in awe of the lessons you gleaned from them.

Days 51-60: Show Compassion

I believe the greatest joy we can experience in our lives is being compassionate to others. When we can extend kindness to someone without expecting anything in return, that is the true definition of love.

The last 10 days likely felt very transformative for you. You should find yourself feeling lighter, clearer, and happier. Now that you are living in this space, you have more energy to put good and love out into the world.

So, in this challenge, your focus is going to be all about how you can show compassion to others. I like to think of this as the "random acts of kindness" challenge in your 90-Day journey.

You are just past the midway point at this stage. We have focused a great deal on your goals, which we will continue to do in the upcoming challenges.

At this time, you are going focus 100 percent on others. I would encourage you to revisit mind-map #2: Love & Give to help you connect with the different ways you want to extend love in your life. Remember we talked about different layers of giving love to yourself, to your inner circle, to your community, and to the world. Look at the latter three and ask yourself what can you do to spread more love in those areas of your life?

For the next 10 days, map out one act of kindness that you can do for either someone you love, someone in your community, or for a larger global cause you care about. The purpose of looking at these different areas is twofold.

1. You will experience how you can express love in many ways in a short amount of time.

2. You will experience a deep joy in giving love unconditionally to the people in your life, as well as to others you don't even know.

These acts of kindness can be large or small, monetary or not. It doesn't depend on the way you express compassion. What matters is purely the act of doing it.

If you're like others who have done the 90-Day Life Challenge, you will find that this period is one of the most fulfilling, because you are putting your entire focus on giving. You will experience such a sense of joy in realizing that the one thing that connects us all is compassion.

If you are good to others, you can create good in this world, and, in turn, good will come back to you.

Days 61-70: Embrace Spontaneity

Every challenge during this 90-day period is designed to pull the proverbial rug out from under you. I am helping you dismantle what you know, what you've grown accustomed to, and what you've gotten comfortable with.

This is all designed to help you get comfortable with getting uncomfortable. Remember, being comfortable means being the same and the same means being stuck. If you're not evolving through life, you're stuck in life.

One of the most pleasurable ways to create instant satisfaction is being spontaneous. At the core of every one of us, what we care most about is freedom. We want the freedom to do the things we want, when we want, and with whom we want. We don't want to get boxed in by rules, routines, opinions, or expectations.

We want the freedom of change. We want the ability to just act without inhibition, and live without fear.

In days 11-20, we focused on the challenge of creating novelty. Now we are going to take that one step further by challenging you to embrace spontaneity.

First, let me make a distinction between the two, because they can be misconstrued as one in the same. They complement each other, yes. To be novel is to be spontaneous, and to be spontaneous is to create something novel.

But novelty is purely the art of doing something new. Spontaneity is the art of doing something new without planning it.

So many things in our lives are scheduled out and pre-planned that we've lost the art of spontaneity, so this challenge is designed to help you feel that spark of just doing things without thinking them through, and allow you to experience the free-spirited side of you.

What you are going to do first is create your "spontaneous toolbox." In this 10-day challenge, you are going to come up with 10 different ways that you can be spontaneous for the next 10 days. Think outside of the box here. Challenge yourself to think of things you can do that will force you to act without inhibition, as in dance like no one is watching and sing like no one is listening.

To be spontaneous means to act without caring what you or others think. I believe this is the true definition of freedom.

Once you have your toolbox in place, the next 10 days are simple enough. Set a reminder on your phone for a different, random time every day with the words "be spontaneous" and do one of those things in your toolbox. Once you've done it, cross it off your list, so that you experience each of the 10 acts of spontaneity over the next 10 days.

What's very fascinating during this challenge is that people will typically start off feeling very self-conscious and unsure on day 1. They don't want to be within earshot of anyone. They feel uncomfortable and insecure. Spontaneity isn't a common practice, so it's naturally going to feel awkward at first. Then, little by little, with each progressive day, you will likely find yourself caring just a little bit less and acting just a little bit more freely.

By the time you reach day 10, you will have revealed a livelier version of you that doesn't question yourself as much as you used to, because you are doing what you want to do in that moment, and it feels amazing.

Days 71-80: Minimize Your Potential Regrets

We have been on an incredible journey so far. With the challenges you have worked through at this point, you have experienced the power of embracing new habits to achieve your goals. You have embraced acting with more personal freedom, and you have celebrated your past as well as putting love out into the world.

That is an amazing feat to accomplish in just 70 days. You should already feel incredibly proud of what you have completed at this stage.

So, I find it appropriate that, as we look to the second-to-last challenge in your 90-day journey, we take the next 10 days and look at anything that could be missing. In the midst of all of the work you have done, I want to make sure that you aren't leaving anything important at this stage of your life on the table.

So, we're going to revisit a core concept from Chapter 4: "Predicting Regrets," and I want you to reflect on the following:

- At this stage, what are you still putting on hold?
- What dream or goal have you yet to take action on?

What matters at this stage is not why you have put it on hold, because you are now focusing on many great things.

What also doesn't matter is that you fully accomplish the very thing you have put on hold in these next 10 days.

What *does matter* is that you start to take action on it now, so that you have momentum to continue to carry out this dream after your 90-Day Life Challenge is complete.

Once you reach Day 90, you will have achieved a new level of growth and satisfaction in your life. That is the big-picture goal. But it's also important to note that this is but a chapter in your life, and that what this challenge should also do for you is catapult your desire to keep evolving and creating the life you want.

So, at this stage, revisit all four of your mind-maps. Go through the list of goals you have set out for yourself and see if there is a goal that stands out. It should be a goal that you haven't put any or little focus on at this stage, but one that you know you need to take action on, otherwise you'll regret it once you hit Day 90.

Most people set an ambitious list of goals on Day 1. It's also common and ok if you don't achieve all of these goals in 90 days. Remember, the point is not to achieve every single possible thing you want to do in your life. It's about giving you the power and the tools you need to live into your dreams at any time in your life, so you don't wake up to regrets later.

Once you have narrowed it down to one of your goals that you want to focus on, ask yourself, "what are 10 simple steps I can do right now over the next 10 days to help me get closer to achieving this goal?"

It's ok for these steps to be simple. I want you to think of this as a progression, just like this entire challenge has been. Your goal during the next 10 days is purely to create momentum. If you end up achieving your goal in 10 days, that's wonderful, but that doesn't have to be the actual goal.

Once you know your 10 steps, schedule them out in your calendar over the next 10 days, so you can focus on completing one step a day.

We simply want to create little wins in micro-commitments, so you remember to keep this dream at the forefront.

Days 81-90: Practice Gratitude

A sunrise...

Your first kiss...

The colors of autumn...

The first steps of an infant...

The first time you tell someone you love them...

All of these things last but for a moment, but think about how amazing you feel when experiencing those moments. We find great joy and great beauty in them. We pause and want the moment to last forever.

We look back on those moments fondly as we move through life, and we'd do anything to relive them again.

Why are these moments so powerful? It's because they create a surge of joy, awe, and love that can feel rare in our day-to-day lives. We crave those feelings. We crave feeling alive, which is why we often live for moments like these.

Far too often, the responsibilities, to-dos, and clutter of everything in life gets in our way and cloud us from seeing the simple joys around us, and prevent us from being grateful for what we have right now.

As we enter the final challenge of your 90-dayjourney, I want to help you see that you have the power to create the same feelings you had in those special moments in every day in your life, by taking a moment to look up and experience what is truly around you.

All through the power of practicing gratitude.

Gratitude has become one of the most pivotal practices in my life and how I have rediscovered the simple joys. When I was on the quest of success through perfection, I found myself always looking ahead to the next thing and the next goal, never seeing what was around me or what I already had in my life. I was also never truly fulfilled. I found myself constantly looking ahead to "what's the next thing, what do I need to do next..."

When I started to practice gratitude, it felt foreign to me, which was a surprise. I have always been a naturally happy person. I have also always been a goal-oriented person, so while I felt a surge of happiness when I achieved a goal, I didn't give myself a deeper sense of appreciation and gratitude for it.

So, for the next 10 days, your focus is simple, yet the benefits you are about to experience will be profound.

Every day to start your day, take a minimum of 10 minutes to think about the things you are grateful for. I find that the most powerful way to do this is to actually write out what you are grateful for. Then once you have finished writing, take a moment and actually read it out loud. It is a really powerful experience to practice gratitude this way, as opposed to just thinking through things in your mind, because you can see the abundance of what you already have in your life.

I personally find that starting the day with this 10-minute gratitude exercise is the most powerful. I'm naturally a morning person, so I feel the most on in the early hours of the day, and writing down my gratitude is like an instant dose of joy. With that being said, another approach is to do this exercise at the end of the day before you go to sleep. You can experiment with both and see what works best for you.

When you start to practice gratitude, you may find yourself trying to find things you are grateful for. Maybe one or two things will pop up at first. Then something powerful happens. The more you practice gratitude on a daily basis, both in the next 10 days as well as after your 90-Day Life Challenge, the more you start to see what has been in front of you this whole time.

When I started to practice gratitude, I would at first think of something successful I did the previous day. It would typically be something purpose- and work-related. But then my eyes started to "see" in a different way... and I became overwhelmed by the wellspring of things I am grateful for.

My health. My family. My friends. My followers. My partner. My dog. My eyes so I can see. My ears so I can hear. The roof over my head. The food at the table. Clean water. Blue skies. Nice people. The clouds. The trees. This life.

All simple joys. All beautiful things. Taken too easily for granted.

I began to see so much of what I already had that it helped me find a new lens for reflecting on my life. One that was built on appreciating everything that I have in the moment, and also being grateful for the journey I am on.

Through this final challenge, you will discover two things:

> One, you will be more grateful for the things you have.

So two, you can be more grateful for the things yet to come. By being grateful for the very things you already have in your life, you will open up the space to attract more of those things into your life.

With gratitude, you put out the energy that you are open to and appreciative of the very thing you've already received.

Without it, you are always on a quest for the next thing, and then wake up wondering why you are constantly in a state of wishing, hoping, and wanting, rather than getting.

Gratitude is where you will find your balance during this challenge, and it is most appropriate at this stage than any other, for it will give you the ability to reflect on the amazing transformation you've created as well as be grateful for what lies ahead for you.

You will get the joy of experiencing both a surge in momentum and a newfound sense of calm and inner peace, because you are focused on the moment in front of you and appreciate each step of the journey.

Gratitude gives you the opportunity to celebrate all that you have, all that you've accomplished, and all that you are.

Take time each day to be grateful for what's in your life. Appreciate the journey and all that it gives you.

CHAPTER 13:

90-DAY SUCCESS PRINCIPLES

"Almost every successful person begins with two beliefs: the future can be better than the present, and I have the power to make it so."

— DAVID BROOKS

TO HAVE A successful 90-Day Life Challenge, you want to be equipped with a set of key principles to use on a daily basis.

The 90-day journey ahead of you is a combination of mindset and strategy, which is why we have addressed both throughout the course of this book, so you have a blueprint of where you are now and what you want to achieve. It's why we have done our due diligence in not only laying out your goals, but also carefully mapping them out in a series of progressive challenges to put these goals into action.

The principles in this chapter will give you a turbocharge for your 90-Day Life Challenge, so you can build added momentum.

Principle #1: Your Mental Means Are Your Most Important Asset

When I started documenting my first 90-Day Life Challenge, one of the first interesting responses I got from one of my followers was, "if only I had the means."

I found that very insightful, because the person who said this looked at this opportunity as requiring a lot of means to make it happen, and she was so focused on this and her own financial limitations that she couldn't see opportunity past them. At the core of it all, what she really believed was: "If I don't have the money, then a better life isn't really possible."

In fairness, there are adventures or goals that you may have in your 90-Day Life Challenge that will require some type of investment, but it's not just an investment in the financial sense, though that's what people often refer to.

Yes, there may be a destination you've been wanting to travel to, or perhaps you have a new business venture that you've been wanting to start. Both of those will require money.

But the money will only take you so far. You need to broaden your definition of "having the means" to something much deeper than what your bank account is telling you. Otherwise you will let your money, or lack thereof, hold you back, no matter how much you want to change your life.

You must also consider your *mental means*.

Your mental means are your fuel behind this journey, not your financial means.

Your mental means are limitless. You can tap into them at any time and in any moment.

It doesn't matter your age, stage of life, career, or net worth. We all have the same capacity to have an abundance of mental means that will be the ultimate driving force to achieve what we want in life.

Your mindset will drive how you think and spend your time, what you believe you're capable of, and what actions you will commit to, which is why we've spent so much time focusing in Sections 1 and 2 of this book on understanding how your mindset is holding you back and what you can do to change it.

It was all to prepare you for this moment, to take action and get past your fears.

Money is nothing, if doubts are holding you back.

Money is only energy, and your current financial situation is oftentimes a reflection of your self-worth.

I say this from both frustrating and liberating experiences. As an entrepreneur, you are responsible for making your own income, and with that responsibility comes great freedom. But I have had a plenty of times where my finances were very tight. Sometimes scary tight. Like in the red and not sure how I was going to pay next month's bills kind of tight.

It was also happening during periods of my life where I felt the worst about myself. I was a hot mess of stress and pressure. I was working my tail off in 12-hour days and still feeling like I could never get my work done or make ends meet. I felt like a complete failure and, no matter what I did, I found myself struggling. My means were depleted in every way possible.

But it wasn't about the quality of work I was doing. It was about the quality of how I felt about myself that was impacting my ability to make a living, or feel like I deserved to make a living.

When I started to focus on my mindset, and literally bombard my brain with affirmations, meditation, and visualization on a multiple-times-a-day basis, I started to see a shift.

My level of work didn't change; in fact, *I worked less.*

Rather than question whether my business strategies would work, I began to trust them. Rather than shrivel up when someone posted a negative comment or criticized me, I moved past it and continued to serve the people I could help. I started to praise myself more and believe more in myself.

By shifting my mindset to more of a space built around belief and positivity, my fortunes began to change. The two types of means are intertwined, but your mental means are at the core. The benefit of focusing on your mental means is that it can lead to a better financial picture for you.

But what this is really about is creating a more confident, joyous, purposeful, and action-oriented version of yourself.

The mental means are what will drive you to success in this challenge.

You can have all the money in the world, but it won't be the key to your growth if you wake up uncertain or full of fear. If you do have the financial means, but your mindset is negative or dis-empowering, this journey will not be fulfilling.

So, as you look ahead to your 90-day journey, ask yourself: "What do you think you are capable of doing?" Knowing that your mental means are limitless, what can you really accomplish, so you can look back and feel fulfilled and complete with who you've become?

This is something we want to have at the end of our lives, and this challenge is an opportunity to start feeling that now, and creating it now, rather than hoping it will happen.

When you put your mental means into practice, abundance will come back to you several times over. Your mental means will be your most important asset, not just in this journey, but throughout the course of the rest of your life.

Principle #2: Focus on Being Present with Yourself, Rather Than Trying to Be Perfect

I used to spend a good deal of my life trying to be perfect. I had always put a lot of pressure on myself since as early as I can remember, because I thought I had to be perfect in order to be successful. I equated feeling pressure with feeling motivated and that the two had to exist together. I also equated feeling pressure with achieving more goals.

In my mind, the more pressure I felt, the more likely it was that I was going to achieve my goals. And the more perfect I was, the better I would feel about myself. But the quest for perfection only led to me finding flaws within myself.

Rather than embrace my successes, I would look to what I did wrong. Rather than celebrate the praise from, or impact I made on, others, I would look to the one person who wasn't satisfied. I was always looking for the squeaky wheel, and I wasted a lot of time and energy in that space.

When I started to embrace impermanence, I got hit in the face with a great wake-up call. I realized that life is short, and time moves fast. What's most important is being present with the time right in front of you and not waste it on distractions, head trash, or procrastination. It's when I started to learn to let go of being perfect, because all it was leading to was putting my big dreams on hold.

I started to realize that perfection only leads to a lack of fulfillment. Criticizing over contentment. Delaying over doing.

The very thing I've been so used to going after (being perfect) was the very thing stopping me from actually doing what I wanted to in life, and becoming who I wanted to be while doing those things.

So, when it comes to your own 90-Day Life Challenge, the goal is to be present with what you want to achieve, but more importantly, who you want to be.

This is a journey. Not just the next 90 days for you, but life itself. It's not about getting it all right, and I'll go so far as to say that it's not about getting it all done. But it's about who you are and how you are showing up in what you do.

Now that might sound like a contradiction in terms, but hear me out.

This is about you being able to wake up in 90 days completely in love with how you are approaching your life and how you feel about yourself. This is not just about doing some checklist and crossing things off and then just going ahead to the next thing.

That's called work. That's called to-dos. That's called looking for the next thing. That's called pressure.

The real satisfaction lies in being present with your journey and seizing the time that lies right in front of you.

Not being so focused on looking forward or looking back that you miss this moment, right now. This is a moment. You. Right Now. Reading these words. Be present with it.

Being present gives you the ability to start to focus again on what you're really thinking. Be present with your own company. Your own company should be the best company you keep, but it is oftentimes the company you neglect.

Be present with the journey ahead of you. Don't quest to be perfect, otherwise you'll only look around and try to find what's missing within yourself.

Being present will make the journey itself the goal.

Principle #3: Be Accountable

This 90-Day Life Challenge is going to be your best accountability partner. Every day is another day to commit to the goals you set out to achieve.

To help you stay on track, take time at least once a week to review your progress on your 90-day goals. Think through the progress you've made in the current challenge you are in. Evaluate what you are doing well and what you could improve upon.

Being accountable in this way will help ensure that this journey is a success for you, while also giving you the chance to course-correct. Because let's face it, there will be challenges, distractions, and off days during this journey. It's ok. Expect them.

But committing time for this every week will be the key to helping you stay on-track and get back on-track when needed. As you grow through the journey, you will discover areas where you can reassess what you need to do and where you need to focus. And if you find that your goals and priorities change through the 90-day period, that's ok too.

What matters the most for you is continued movement forward. Keep pushing. Keep growing, and keep striving to be a better version of yourself than you were the day before. Celebrate the small steps as well as the big milestones that you achieve throughout this journey.

If you miss a goal or fall behind on your schedule during the next 90 days, brush it off and start again the next day. You can always create an opportunity to reassess and reset your plan. Focus on that rather than being hard on yourself if you miss a goal.

Accountability is all about keeping your eyes focused forward. If you become your best accountability partner, no matter what you set out to accomplish, you will be successful, because in the end you accomplished the most important thing, and that's pushing yourself.

Principle #4: Visualize Daily

There is nothing more powerful than letting your mind see what it is that you want to create.

You have the ability to be and do anything you want. The key to getting there is picturing the very thing you want to accomplish in your mind before it even happens.

Your mind can experience the same feelings, emotions, and actions by you envisioning something, just as if it has actually happened.

As an example, picture right now holding on orange in your hand. Imagine feeling the texture of the rind in that orange as you roll it around your fingers. Now start to peel away some of that rind and smell the burst of orange scent coming into your nose.

You *can* smell the orange, can't you? All by just picturing it in your mind.

Your mind is that powerful. If you use it to visualize what you want to accomplish during your 90-Day Life Challenge, then you will set the stage for creating it, because you've already seen it and experienced it.

So, every day in the next 90 days, take at least five minutes to visualize the end-result in your mind. Think about what it will feel like at Day 90, having accomplished the goals you have set out for yourself. Picture what you are doing, how you are feeling, and what your life will look like at that time.

As you envision it, you create the reality and future that's just waiting for you.

If you need something to support what you're picturing, get a poster board and put up photos and sayings of things that symbolize the transformation you want to create in your 90-Day Life Challenge, so that you can look at this board during your daily visualization to reinforce your goals.

Perception is reality, and by creating the reality in your own mind and the vision of it within you, you will be able to create it in your life.

YOUR TIME IS NOW

You are now ready to embark on your 90-Day Life Challenge.

Together we have focused on reflecting on your life now, and setting new priorities for the life you want to create.

So you can build your path to take action on your dreams now, and no longer put them on hold.

Thank you for the opportunity to guide you into the next chapter of your life. Here is to an amazing transformation ahead.

A SPECIAL INVITATION FOR YOU

Everything I do in my life today is built from a place of helping people build their lives now, so they don't wake up to regrets later.

It's why I created the 90-Day Life Academy, so I can help people break away from feeling burned out in life and feel on purpose again, offering people even greater support during their journey.

If you would like to learn more about how to rebuild your life in 90 days, then I encourage you to check out my 90-Day Life Academy. I promise you that it will be the catalyst to creating a more fulfilling, more rewarding life.

If you're interested in the program, I've created a free video training series that will teach you even more about how to rebuild your life in 90 days. I'll also give you more information on the academy.

Check out the video training series here:
http://90daylifebook.com/free-video-training

Regardless of whether you want to join me in the 90-Day Life Academy, I want to hear your success stories!

I hope you will send me a note when you start your 90-Day Life Challenge, telling me how you are doing and how your life has changed as a result of doing it.

You can reach me at **hello@drjenfaber.com**.

Thank you for the opportunity to inspire you. I look forward to being a part of your continued journey.

Dr. Jen

ADDITIONAL RESOURCES

If you want more in-depth, step-by-step guidance to rebuild your life in 90 days, check out the following additional resources at:

90DayLifeBook.Com/Resources

Get the audiobook version of The 90 Day Life here: **90daylifebook.com/audiobook**

Get the accompanying workbook for The 90 Day Life here: **90daylifebook.com/workbook**

Get my free video training series that will teach you even more about how to rebuild your life in 90 days here: **90daylifebook.com/free-video-training**

A SMALL ASK

Thank You for Reading My Book!

I appreciate all your feedback, and I love hearing what you have to say.

I need your input to make the next version of this book, and my future books, better.

Please leave me a helpful review on Amazon letting me know what you thought of the book.

Thanks so much!

Dr. Jen Faber

WITH GRATITUDE

It is with heartfelt gratitude, and a deep desire to share, that I simply could not have done this journey alone. I am so appreciative of everyone who has supported me, my book, and its launch throughout every stage of the journey.

Thank you to everyone who has been a part of bringing this book to life. Because of you, you have helped me say yes to my dreams and get my message out to people all over the world.

I am forever grateful for you.

ABOUT THE AUTHOR

DR. JEN FABER, D.C., is a lifestyle entrepreneur and coach who empowers people to break away from burnout in life to living the life of their dreams.

She started her career as a chiropractor and built a thriving six-figure house call practice, then transitioned to coaching over 5,000 health and wellness professionals out of practice burnout. Now she is focusing on expanding her mission and message into the personal growth and motivation space, so she can inspire more people around the world.

Recognized as one of the "Top 10 Wellness Leaders to Watch" by Longevity Media, Dr. Jen focuses on teaching unconventional ways to think, dream, and live, by breaking past fear and doubt, so people can take advantage of the time right in front of them, rather than put their lives on hold.

To learn more, visit **www.drjenfaber.com.**

REFERENCES

1. https://www.marketwatch.com/story/5-reasons-americans-are-unhappy-2015-10-12

2. Pepper, T. (2015, April 15). Why Millennials Are in for a Worse Midlife Crisis than their Parents. Retrieved from **http://time.com/money/3665682/millennials-midlife-crisis**

3. **Ibid**

4. Blanchflower, D.G., Oswald, A.J. (2008, April). Is well-being U-shaped over the life cycle? Retrieved from **http://www.sciencedirect.com/science/article/pii/S0277953608000245**

5. Ware, B. (2016, August 21). Regrets of the Dying. Retrieved from **http://www.bronnieware.com/blog/regrets-of-the-dying**

6. **http://www.nytimes.com/2012/02/14/science/novelty-seeking-neophilia-can-be-a-predictor-of-well-being.html**

7. Gallagher, W. (2011, December 29). Understanding Our Need for Novelty and Change. Retrieved from **https://www.amazon.com/New-Understanding-Need-Novelty-Change/dp/1594203202**

8. Carver, R.P., Johnson, R.L., Friedman, H.L. (1971, March 1). Factor Analysis of the Ability to Comprehend Time-Compressed Speech.

Retrieved from **http://journals.sagepub.com/doi/ abs/10.1080/10862967109546974**

9. Dr. Merzenich, M., Dr. Doidge, N. (2008, July). What is Brain Plasticity? Retrieved from **https://www. brainhq.com/brain-resources/brain-plasticity/ what-is-brain-plasticity**

10. Forbes Coaches Council (2017, August 31). 15 Signs You've Hit Your Mid-Life Crisis (And What to Do About It). Retrieved from **https://www.forbes.com/ sites/forbescoachescouncil/2017/08/31/15-signs- youve-hit-your-mid-life-crisis-and-what-to-do- about-it/**

11. **https://www.sciencealert.com/here-s-how-long- it-takes-to-break-a-habit-according-to-science**

12. Lally, P., van Jaarsveld, C.H.M., Potts, H.W.W., Wardle, J. (2009, July 16). How are Habits Formed: Modelling Habit Formation in the Real World. Retrieved from **http://onlinelibrary.wiley.com/doi/10.1002/ ejsp.674/abstract**

13. Luciani, J. (2015, December 29). Why 80 Percent of New Year's Resolution Fail. Retrieved from **https:// health.usnews.com/health-news/blogs/eat-run/ articles/2015-12-29/why-80-percent-of-new- years-resolutions-fail**